Finally Home
Lessons on Life from a Free-Spirited Dog

Written by Elizabeth Parker

Author's Note:

Please note that this book is not meant to be utilized as a training manual, nor is it meant to advise on how to train any dog. Please follow the instructions of a professional dog trainer if you are seeking assistance, as the dog-training conventions used in this book may not be suitable for other dogs. In addition, please check with your veterinarian before administering any drugs, food, snacks or drinks to your dog that are mentioned in this book. Thank you.

Thank you to my husband for having the courage to adopt Buddy and the patience to deal with his goofy antics. Special thanks for all of your support and advice while I wrote this. You're a great Daddy to the pups and we are lucky to have you in our lives.

To Buddy, Brandi and Toffee- Thanks for being such special, lovable and funny dogs. I'm looking forward to some more funny adventures with you and your Dad!

Thank you to my editor, Michael Simon, for spending so many grueling hours going through this story and pointing out my errors and inconsistencies.

Table of Contents

Introduction

"...My first encounter with Buddy was at a festive New Year's Eve party. I was dressed in my best outfit purchased specifically for this occasion while enjoying a delicious, freshly-mixed cocktail of vodka, cranberry, and lots of ice. While involved in typical party conversation, I did not focus on anything else in the room around me, nor did I think it was necessary. I have to admit I did see him out of the corner of my eye, but it was just too late. I didn't think he would actually do it, but there it was—that look in his eye and all-too-satisfying smirk on his face. There was absolutely nothing I could do. I tried to move out of the way, but it all happened way too fast. I went from standing up enjoying a drink and remarkable conversation, to having my mid-section pummeled by this giant ball of fur. He already had my free hand in his mouth pulling me down, tail wagging one hundred miles per hour, and I was now wearing my delicious drink on my brand new clothes. Before I could gain my composure, Buddy was already off to the next victim..."

— (coworker, upon first meeting Buddy)

There is a time in most people's lives when they have been emotionally inspired or amazed by something that was completely unexpected. Sometimes it is so touching that they want to share their experience with the world and tell their story.

This particular story is about a precious heart along with a free-spirited little boy who owns that heart. This little boy has expressive brown eyes, a beautiful smile, and a golden-brown coat that he never takes off. He also has a huge pinkish-brown nose and four very fast legs. His name is Buddy. He answers to that…when he wants to.

Chapter 1-Summer of '99

Each plan in life is derived from a single idea. Some ideas start in the least expected of places during the least likely of times. When an idea snowballs and takes on a life of its own—that is when it becomes a reality.

It is safe to say that it all started when I was employed at a sunglass manufacturer as an Electronic Data Interchange Specialist. This is just a sophisticated title for someone who monitors the electronic transactions between the manufacturer and retail stores. It was a pleasurable job, one where you did not need to dress in uncomfortable business attire, and though the salary was not great, it was somewhat respectable.

The people were fun, the bosses were friendly, the office was clean, and, for the most part, it was a fairly decent job. It was here that I met my husband, Michael; we began dating approximately two years after I started my employment there in the summer of 1999. It was the typical story of two goofy twenty-something-year-olds with the same wise-ass mentality, the same principles and views on life, and, in Michael's words (or pick-up line), we were both half-orphans. He had lost his mom to breast cancer when he was at the tender age of four. I had lost my dad to a job-related illness shortly after I turned nine years old.

In the year 2000, after working at the company for three years, I decided to make a drastic change and start looking for a new occupation. Although I loved the job and the line of work, rumors were circulating that our office was in the midst of closing down. I figured I had better be prepared and search for something just in case.

After reading the classifieds and modifying my résumé and cover letter over fifty times, I was offered a job as an assistant producer for a popular local news station's weekend program. Even though the decision was a bit intimidating at first, I had reluctantly given my resignation letter to my previous employer, said my good-byes, and started my journey on a new career path.

As luck would have it, just as I had begun to get acclimated and understand all aspects of the job including the software, technology, procedures, office politics, etc., I received news that this job was closing its doors, as well!

Needless to say, I was beginning to get a bit of a complex. I noticed a pattern and figured this time it would be wise to conduct some extensive research before moving on to my next area of employment.

After sitting at my computer and sifting through tons of verbose ads offering employment in various fields, I submitted my résumé to what I felt was going to be a respectable and stable employer. I researched the company on the Internet, carefully read through their complex website, and thought I had plenty of concrete detail to support my belief that this job lead was solid.

The company had been in business for over twenty years and had multiple offices scattered throughout the country. I did not see any obvious red flags waving in my direction.

Needless to say, after interviewing with half of the knowledgeable staff in the technology department and making numerous visits to their office, I was finally offered the job. I was scheduled to start a little later that summer and looked forward to it. It was about time!

It was during these various job transitions that Michael and I were growing a bit closer in our relationship and discussing the possibility of living together. I was still residing at my mother's house, however, and he owned his own home.

After some lengthy conversations, we had also started toying with the idea of adopting a dog, more specifically a golden retriever. We had both fallen in love with their friendly, amusing temperament. For the most part in the beginning we would just take quick browses through puppy stores only to walk out a few minutes later. We were, after all, only toying with the idea. We were not even living together yet, so we were uncertain if were ready for the sound of padded feet running through the house and through our lives.

During that same time period, a coworker of mine was making conversation and coincidentally asked me if I knew anyone who would be interested in adopting a dog. I wanted to raise my hand, jump up and down, and scream out "Yes, me!" I managed to refrain from making a spectacle of myself, but instead tried to act cool without displaying too much enthusiasm. Of course, I couldn't leave without trying to find out some information about the dog.

"What type of dog is it? Ah, how old? Hmm, why are they getting rid of it? Boy or girl? Does it bite? Is it housebroken? Hey…what is the dog's name?"

He was not certain of the specifics at that precise moment in time and probably did not realize that he was talking to an obsessed dog fanatic. He advised me that he would make it a point to speak to his friend and find out more detailed information. He also offered to describe a brief reenactment of his first encounter with this dog at a party his friends had thrown (quoted in the introduction of this book). Incidentally, I figured he was exaggerating.

I got a surge of excitement about the idea and then quickly calmed myself down, meandered back to my desk, and tried to keep my mind focused on work. I did not think much more of it until I went home later that evening.

That night during dinner, I spoke to my future husband and casually mentioned the conversation that I'd had with my coworker with no real intention of going to meet this dog. I did have my coworker's

phone number just in case, but I didn't think we w̶
entertain the idea as we already had so much going o̶
in our lives already.

After discussing it for a while, though, we
weighed the pros and cons and figured out a solution
for each possible obstacle that we could think of. We
reviewed our budget, our future together, dog sitters,
work schedules, hours the dog would be left alone, and
many other topics regarding responsible dog
ownership. After a couple of hours, we made a
decision.

"Why not?" We agreed. Let's just find out more
about him. We figured there was no harm in inquiring
about the dog without making any real commitment.

After we cleaned the dishes and returned them to
their allotted sections of the cupboard, we called my
coworker that very night. As it turned out, he was
going to be visiting this same friend's house anyway
and we would be able to get all of the answers that we
needed about the dog. We were still in the research
stage and had no concrete plans of adopting until we
knew more. A healthy dog could live as long as
eighteen years or sometimes even longer, and it was
definitely a strong commitment.

We called anyhow and asked all of the relevant
questions. We discovered it was a purebred golden
retriever. Coincidentally, this was the exact breed we
had been seeking.

Both my cousin and a friend of ours had owned
this type of puppy, and we absolutely loved it. From
both parties we knew that the breed was best known
for their well-behaved and goofy temperament in

beautiful, golden coat and
s.

one was about a year and a half and
s up to date on his shots, neutered,
housebroken, and did not bite. His owner informed us,
"His name…is Buddy."

Buddy. We had to see him even just to play with
him for a little while. Why would anyone give him up?
That was the nagging question. There had to be
something else going on. This opportunity was too
good to be true. No one in his or her right mind would
voluntarily give up a beautiful, young, and healthy
golden retriever. After speaking with the dog's owner,
we made plans to go see him over the upcoming
weekend.

That Sunday morning, we woke up early and
stopped for some breakfast at the town diner down the
block before making our way to the dog owner's home
in Long Island. As we drove down the tree-lined cul-
de-sac, we pulled up to a beautiful, large Victorian
house and parked our car at the bottom of the circular
driveway.

Two young children greeted us at the door, and
their mom trailed promptly behind them. We
introduced ourselves and explained that we were there
to meet the pup. The mother seemed friendly enough
as she led us down the stairs to the secluded basement.
We would soon find out that this was Buddy's only
room.

As we descended, we immediately noticed Buddy.
He was utterly breathtaking, and it was easy to fall in
love instantly. He was in the corner by himself quietly

minding his own business and chewing on his slim rawhide bone. That is until his ears perked up and he looked toward the stairs with his adorable eyes to notice us walking toward him.

Have you ever been in the ocean when the waves were so high you could not keep afloat, and it seemed like every time you caught your breath another wave came to knock you over? This is the best way I could describe Buddy's initial reaction to us.

With his rawhide bone dangling out of his mouth, he started barking as soon as he caught eyes with us and then ran and jumped on us as if he'd never seen people before. For those of you who are familiar with that golden retriever smile, it was broader than I had ever seen. He kept tossing the bone up in the air a little bit, not quite letting go, but not quite wanting to hold it. He was indecisive about whether he should keep his bone or bark…so balancing the bone between his teeth, he did both. He was absolutely overjoyed.

We still could not comprehend why these people were getting rid of this bundle of love. His fluffy tail was wagging a million miles per hour and he was completely in his element. All this dog wanted to do was love and be loved. It was written all over his furry face. He was absolutely beautiful.

He developed this incredible tone in his voice that was not quite a cry, not truly a bark, but something in between. With his bone still in his mouth, he uttered a noise I had never heard before, which would soon become known as his trademark "Buddy-bark."

To describe it would be somewhat ridiculous, and I am certain that spell check will not like it, but I will give it a whirl. It sounded something like "a woo woo woo woooo wooooooooooo," the last "woo" carrying a somewhat higher, more intense, uneven pitch than the others.

As the owner struggled to control Buddy, she attached his chewed-up leather leash to his collar and began to give us some background on him. We could immediately tell that she was desperate to find him a home and that she had no control over this dog whatsoever.

She explained that they had tried to surrender him to Golden Retriever Rescue, but there was an extremely long waiting list and there was no room yet for Buddy. She was already his second and then his third owner.

His first owner had given him up because he was way too big for a small apartment. The current owners admitted that they had also given him up to someone who promptly returned him a day later. They regretted that they could not handle him and exclaimed "good luck!" as they returned him.

If we did decide to adopt him, we would essentially be his fourth owners. "If" being the operative word. If we did not take him, they were going to have to surrender him to a shelter. They were running out of choices.

The owners did the right thing by trying to find him a good home, but unfortunately they'd had no luck in their search. People had come to meet him and were immediately turned off by his neurotic mannerisms and excessive barking. He was getting too difficult to manage, and they were ready to give him up. It was the

usual sad unwanted puppy story; his time w.
essentially running out.

Different shelters follow different rules, but there are some kill shelters that give the dog a certain period of time until they get adopted. If they exceed that limitation, they are put to sleep. There are just too many stray dogs and not enough facilities or financial means to accommodate all of them.

We needed to uncover what the catch was. He must have been vicious, and they were just not telling us. Or perhaps he had some extreme medical condition that they did not want to disclose to us. He appeared to be healthy and seemed like a normal yet overly energetic year-and-a-half-old pup. He did not act ferocious, although some dogs do tend to show their true temperament under different circumstances.

We asked some more specific questions, such as how he was with kids, dogs, men, women, etc. To all questions, she answered pretty much the same thing. He was "fine, never had a vicious episode, just a bit hyper."

We inquired about his behavior while he was on walks and how he acted in the car. She answered that she did not know as they never got the chance to take him for either.

He was let out in their backyard but did not have the ability to run around at all to stretch his legs because there was no fence around the yard. On an average day, he was walked back there on a leash to do his business and then was immediately put back in the lonely and dark basement.

questioning her on the personality of this
u...... . wondering what his main issues were, we
were still not seeing the entire picture. We pressed on a
little more to solve the mystery. He was definitely an
excitable dog, but we figured it was only because he
was happy to see new people.

She simply explained that they were giving him up
because she and her husband worked long hours. It
was difficult to entertain this dog after a long workday.
In addition, he chewed a lot and jumped a lot.

"He jumps on the kids. He jumps on company. He
knows his commands but does not obey them. He eats
a variety of things that he should not be eating."

She recalled how they came across him eating the
children's building blocks, crayons, and other objects
they could not identify. He was a little wild and a lot
out of control, so they had him on medication to calm
him down—sort of like a puppy Prozac. He was a year
and a half, still more or less a puppy.

The puzzle was slowly beginning to get pieced
together. A puppy locked in the basement for twelve
lonely hours each day without any chance to run free
or release his energy. Hmm, wouldn't you have acted
the same way?

We were there long enough to take notice of their
futile attempts at training techniques. When he jumped,
they gave him a treat to get him down. When he
mouthed us or anything else, they gave him a treat to
remove his mouth.

We recognized an immediate pattern. The owners
did what they thought was right in getting Buddy to
behave. What they did not count on was that this dog

was highly intelligent and realized exactly what to
to get a treat. Knowing this, he did the things he go
rewarded for doing: good or bad.

Many unsuspecting owners might have done the
same thing. It is a common mistake, and it happens all
too often. You can't fault someone if they are not used
to dealing with an incredibly smart dog. The problem
is that when a person tries to train an intelligent dog,
the dog will easily learn how to manipulate any
situation to get precisely whatever it is that they want.

The hard truth is that a dog acts the way that it
does because it was actually trained to behave in that
manner. Most people cannot accept this fact, but it is
true. If you've had a dog since it was a puppy, you are
the only master, aside from its birth mother, that the
dog has ever known.

Unquestionably, this was the case with Buddy. He
associated committing these bad behaviors with getting
some yummy doggy treats! He was not necessarily a
"bad" dog. He was just doing what he learned and
interpreted in his little, intelligent mind to be "good"
things.

After a few more enjoyable moments of sitting on
the cold floor with this charming, playful pup, we
thanked the couple for allowing us to visit with Buddy
and went on our way.

Covered head to toe in dog hair and a good portion
of doggy drool, we walked up the stairs and out of the
house into the frigid December air. Buddy had been
jumping and clinging to us on our way out, and we
could still hear his desperate barking as the door closed
behind us. I was thinking, "No way." There was no

easible way we would be able to accommodate the needs of this crazy, disobedient dog. I was already onto my next thought of what to do for the remainder of the day and not even thinking that adopting him was a remote possibility.

When we reached the bottom of the driveway, I playfully posed the question to Michael. I just wanted to gauge his reaction and wholeheartedly expected him to laugh.

"So, what do you think?"

His answer was the complete opposite of what I was expecting. "Absolutely, let's adopt him."

When I heard his response, I got a bit lightheaded and immediately started to have a lack of confidence in my dog-training ability. To say I was stunned would be an understatement. I never predicted that would be his answer. I looked at Michael to try and determine if he were serious. Why was he joking like this?

I love all dogs, regardless of the breed, but Michael had never owned a dog. I thought this dog of all dogs would be a complete turn-off. I envisioned Michael's "starter dog" to be somewhat calm, well-behaved, and easy to manage.

Instead, his reply was, "Let's call them first thing tomorrow to let them know we will adopt him."

While I was undoubtedly thrilled with the idea, I still had my concerns about handling such a crazed animal. Growing up, we had many family dogs, but I was the youngest in the family and never spent time training them. They just always seemed well-behaved. I usually spent time playing with them and never questioned it. This would be my first real test at responsibility, and we would have to figure out how train him. He would not just "magically" becom obedient. Was I up for the proposed challenge? Was Michael?

Still in awe and feeling mixed emotions of joy and trepidation, I made the phone call once we got home rather than waiting until the next morning. With an obvious tremble in my voice, I let them know that we would happily adopt Buddy. Little did I know that one phone call would be the one that changed our lives.

We made plans to pick him up on Thursday evening after work. I could not ascertain why, but I was nervous all week and could not wait to get him. I felt like I was expecting a baby—albeit an eighty-pound baby with lots of fur, but a baby nonetheless. I was also extremely happy. I don't think I slept at all that week!

I recall that I had stopped at a local pet store prior to his adoption and walked up and down the aisles in a cosmic daze. Without knowing what he liked, I picked up a small bag of food, a variety of treats, stuffed animals, and various squeaky toys of different shapes and sizes. I could not concentrate in anticipation of adopting this crazed pup.

We cleaned the entire house and doggy-proofed it the best that we could. We had it all meticulously planned out. Michael, his niece, and I were going to take two cars. Michael would drive home in his car with the crate and all of Buddy's belongings. Michael's niece and I would drive home with Buddy. We would then have a few quality hours to spend with m during the night. What do they say about the best laid plans?

Chapter 2-Thursday December 21st, 2000

The shortest day of the year. The official Winter Solstice. The longest drive home. The day Michael and I officially became insane.

That evening, we arrived at Buddy's house, and to our surprise, his owners were not home. Instead, one of their relatives was there waiting for us. She was very kind and gave us all of Buddy's toys, food, treats, blankets, and his crate at no charge. She went over his feeding schedule with us as well as the commands that he knew. She showed us his veterinary papers proving he was up to date with all of his shots and gave us some other papers, including the name of his breeder, his first owner, the toys he liked, and other random information. This dog probably cost them close to a thousand dollars (if not more), yet they were giving him away for free, along with all of his belongings.

We asked if she would like us to wait for the owners and their kids to come home so that they could officially say goodbye to him. Her answer was pretty firm.

"No. Buddy probably would not even recognize them to say goodbye." We stared at her for a minute or two in disbelief. We then caught on and understood. This family was just happy to let him go. We found it a bit disheartening that his own family would not say goodbye, not even the kids, and our hearts immediately went out to him. We had said our brief good-byes to the woman, received some hand-written instructions, a few more veterinary papers…and Buddy.

I do commend them for their sincere effort in searching for a home for him and making sure his health was not neglected in the interim. Some people have been known to dump their unwanted dog in some remote area, left by themselves to fend for food, shelter, and protection, or even worse. At least these owners ensured that his required veterinary visits were followed.

As we ascended the basement stairs en route to the car, Buddy did not seem to have a care that he was leaving. He hopped the steps two at a time, all the while panting, tugging on the leash, and wagging his fluffy tail. This all seemed to be a good time to him…or maybe he just knew something that we did not.

We loaded Buddy's belongings in Michael's car and put Buddy in the back seat of my car. I had owned many dogs growing up so I was quite used to driving with them as passengers. This was not going to be any different—or at least that is what I thought. I never seriously contemplated it until I actually made my first attempt to drive with Buddy.

I had driven approximately fifteen feet when I w. forced to stop my car right there in the middle of the road without any warning. Michael stopped next to me in his car and looked at me, curious to find out what in the world would cause me to just stop like that.

That is, until he noticed the eighty-pound dog with his paws wrapped securely around my neck from the back. I simply could not move. The only choice I had was to stop. I could not even turn the steering wheel.

Buddy was so excited that he was jumping back and forth from the back seat into the front seat onto our laps, and he wrapped his two front paws around my neck giving me the biggest bear hug he could muster. Lesson learned: *Do not ever doubt the strength of golden retrievers.*

With that, once we peeled Buddy's huge paws from my neck, we had to resort to an unplanned, but very necessary Plan B.

Michael parked his car on the side of the road and got into my back seat to control Buddy. This is where we learned that the words "control" and "Buddy" were never to be used in the same sentence again. It simply would never work out that way. These were only the first few of many lessons learned by owning an overly rambunctious, highly intelligent, eighty-pound golden retriever. I was slowly starting to understand the very reason it was not easy to place this dog in any sane home. I suppose people that were in their right minds recognized that this overexcited dog was insane.

That was our initial thought at that point as well. Our second thought was, "Hey, let's just put him back in their yard and take off. They will notice he is there ome time tonight, and they can go back to the tedious job of finding him a home."

We sat there and stared at each other, trying to read each other's thoughts while dreadfully listening to Buddy's exhilarated panting as he jumped from seat to seat and from person to person. After toying with the idea of returning Buddy, we decided against it. Though—make no mistake—we still had our doubts.

The ride home was not enjoyable one bit. Emotions were flying high: anxiety, lack of common sense, dread, and a severe sense of regret. We lived about twenty to thirty minutes from Bud's old home. Typically on an average day after rush hour, you could jump on the expressway and drive about fifty-five to sixty miles per hour. I think I broke every traffic law that night and made it home in exactly twelve minutes.

The last thing I remember about that wearisome car ride was that my soon-to-be husband was literally wearing Buddy as a fur hat. Buddy had managed to climb up and balance himself between the rear window and the top of Michael's head so that the only thing I was able to see in my rearview mirror was this pup's enormous body. I could barely make out Michael underneath all of that golden fur. The only evidence that he was still back there was the occasional sound of him yelling, "drive faster!"

The single possible chance of making it home alive was based on giving Buddy treats, following the destructive pattern that had been the foundation for his bad behavior. We fed him an entire jar of treats in those long twelve minutes. I truly believe that Buddy was merely testing us to see how long it would take for us to emotionally break down as his previous owners had done.

It was an exhausting night to say the least. We still had to drive back and get Buddy's crate. There was no way we were going to let this pup roam free at his leisure during his first night. I had picked the short straw and ventured back out into the cold December night to get Buddy's crate while Michael and his niece made their first courageous attempt to train Bud.

Chapter 3-A New Life

Being a hero to someone, even if it is a dog, is a feeling like no other. Though it can be frustrating, it can be the most rewarding thing to give someone a second chance at a happy life.

On his first night exploring his new home, Bud ran through the house at record speed, showing joy in discovering new sights, new smells, and—unbeknownst to us—new ways to get into trouble. He was definitely housebroken which was a benefit to us, but at this point, we were convinced that this dog never slept or even napped for that matter!

He had a highly excessive amount of energy. He was friendly as could be, but with what seemed to be trampolines attached to the soft pads of his huge feet, he delved into everything. I had never experienced a dog jumping and frolicking as much as he did. He wanted to investigate every corner of our house, and we did not mind that at all as it was expected, but he was beyond insane with the amount of liveliness he possessed. We figured that he was just overwhelmed, and after a few more minutes of exploring, he would grow tired and eventually calm down.

We figured wrong. After a few arduous hours of trying to keep up with him, he was not even close to relenting yet we had no choice but to go to sleep. Our dialog was no longer making any sense, and our eyes were already closing as we robotically walked up the staircase.

We put him in his old, broken-down silver crate with his own torn-up blankets and a bunch of his toys. We then kissed him good-night and hoped for the best. Every time we would go check on him, he was wide awake. Three days might have passed before we noticed that he even closed his eyes for more than a blink.

Our hearts went out to him as he must have been so confused. No one had ever taken the time to bond with him and make him feel safe.

During the days that followed, we were forced to make snap decisions regarding the training of this dog. One of the things we decided on was that we were going to take him off of the "calming" medicine that he had been given. We promptly flushed the remaining three bottles down the toilet. We were not going to have a healthy, active puppy on downers. There was just no way; we would much rather take our chances.

As crazy as he was, he certainly wasn't sick. There was no reason for his personality to be altered by drugs. The pills did not seem to do anything to help calm him down anyway, so what was the point? We were determined to make this work out no matter what the consequences. We were confident that we wou figure out ways to calm him down.

It was an exciting adventure and the perfect time to adopt him. Christmas was literally around the corner, in four days to be exact, and we were looking forward to it. We were thrilled to celebrate this new addition to our family.

Underneath the Christmas tree were a wide variety of toys ranging from chew toys to stuffed animals, tennis balls to bones, squeaky toys to Buster Cubes, and everything in between. He had his own toy chest filled to the brim within a few short days.

On Christmas Day we locked him in the bedroom for a few minutes while we set each toy (wrapped, of course) in the middle of the living room. You would have thought we had ten young children by the look of it.

When all of the toys were perfectly arranged, we opened the door, and Buddy burst out of the bedroom like a freight train to discover his new treasures. He was so excited and did not know what to do first. The expression on his face showed pure elation.

He opened some of the wrapping with some help from us and took each toy in his mouth, threw it up in the air, shook his head back and forth, and then jumped around in a circle before moving onto the next one. Sometimes he grabbed one and performed his trademark somersault move, in which he would actually tumble over while tucking his head and all. He then held the toy with his two front paws, inviting us to join in the celebration.

Watching him was the highlight of our Christmas. He seemed to love each and every toy. We hoped he would realize he could finally relax; he was finally home.

After playing with all of his toys over and over again, he carefully selected which one he wanted to stick with for a while. The first one he chose to play with was his rawhide. We were thankful as this would keep him busy for some time and we could finally relax. After a few minutes, we soon noticed that he had a unique and amusing habit with rawhide bones, at least from what I had previously witnessed watching other dogs.

Most dogs upon receiving a rawhide went off into their private corner or even outside and could not wait to devour it. Buddy, on the other hand, ventured off to another room by himself and after about three minutes, we heard him bark and yelp.

Without knowing what he was up to in there, I was able to strategically sneak up on him one day (which was never easy to do) and see what was making him so vocal. When I walked in, I tried to contain my laughter as I noticed that he had messed up all of the covers on the bed, buried his bone in the covers, and then retrieved it again.

He repeated this numerous times until he noticed I was there. When he caught me watching him, he vocalized his "Buddy-bark" and then zipped past me. This was not so different, as a lot of dogs did attempt to bury bones every once in a while.

What was different was that if we chose not to go see what he was up to in those three minutes, he would come running out full speed, again reciting his notorious Buddy-bark, and invite us to chase him. He acted so goofy, running through open doors, around tables, up stairs, down stairs, and all over the house.

If we stopped chasing him, he would come and try to entice us to play some more. To Buddy, it was never about eating the bone. The bone would last him months. All he wanted to do was grab our attention and play with us.

Luckily, he would never bite. We could put our mouth on one end of the bone (not that we would ever really want to), but he would not even growl. Instead he would just move over so that we could join him…that is, if we could catch him.

As hyper as he was, we loved spending time with him. Spoiling him was so much fun. While his previous owners did not beat him, they neglected him and that was a form of abuse, even though I do not believe that was their intention. This particular golden thrived on attention as well as plenty of exercise, so locking him in the basement was one of the worst things they could have done.

They fed him well enough and gave him plenty of toys and shelter, but second to food, Buddy needed constant love, and his mind needed intense challenges daily. We wanted to make sure this dog never had to know loneliness again…and he hasn't. Come to think of it, neither have we.

This was just the beginning. As it turned out, we hadn't even touched the surface of the many mischievous and embarrassing situations we would encounter while learning to train Buddy. We had no dea about what we were in for or the challenges we were about to face.

Chapter 4-Getting to Know Each Other

Things are not always what they seem. Sometimes a little perseverance and a lot of patience can work wonders. Look into the heart of the issue and it is there that you will find your true answer.

Since we had already established that Buddy was not an ordinary dog, we decided to hit the bookstore and grasp some knowledge about how to handle such a unique type of pup.

Most of the training books noted that the key to handling a rambunctious dog was variety and plenty of exercise, so we made sure that we adhered to those guidelines. It did not matter. None of this helped. We went through tons of books by various authors.

Desperate, we attempted a variety of training techniques, and we asked anyone who knew *anything* about dogs more than enough questions.

At the vet, we begged for any advice they could give us. We asked them to evaluate Buddy. They agreed he was exceptionally hyper. Maybe even a little over the top. They did not see anything physically wrong with him, but with a slight hesitation they all admitted that he was a bit out of the norm.

One of the vets even claimed that she recognized him. She told us that he was in training (which he was prior to our adopting him) and that they had given him multiple aggression tests which he had passed with flying colors. The tests consisted of instructing Buddy to sit next to a person while he was leashed for a long period of time. The purpose of this was to evaluate his reaction

They analyzed his temperament under many different circumstances to see if any annoyance was exhibited. For example, they noted his reaction when they took away his food, bones, and other various things of "importance" to him. These procedures were used to assess if he had any issues with resource guarding, which is when dogs show possessiveness or aggression over their food, toys or bones. It is a difficult issue to correct, as it is completely normal for a dog, especially in the wild.

Each and every time, Buddy wagged his tail. There was not an ounce of aggression in this dog.

We did, however, have Buddy's temperament questioned at one specific point in time. One of our veterinarians, with whom we generally had a great relationship, gave Buddy a big red X on his file and required that we administer a tranquilizer any time we were to bring him in. We could not believe he was referring to our dog.

How could they think that Buddy, of all dogs, was ferocious? When we inquired about what brought this on, we found out that it stemmed from a specific episode that had occurred during one of his visits.

A frightened veterinary technician took Buddy into the back room and was trying to examine him during a routine check-up when he got up and "lunged" at her.

While this may sound horrifying, if you know dogs and you saw Buddy, you would understand that his version of lunging was nothing more than trying to trample you to the ground so that he could wrestle with you and play. He was never malicious.

If someone was holding the leash and then backed away—to Buddy—this was a major invite to have some fun. He really did not care if you could keep up with him or not. Apparently this technician could not. I do not fault her, however, as not many people could.

The vet explained that if he had personally witnessed the whole thing and if they had been outside playing, he would not have been alarmed. They had to exercise caution, however, as some of the friendliest dogs could turn temporarily vicious while visiting the vet.

While this is definitely true, we explained that this was nothing more than Buddy being Buddy, and again if you knew him, you would understand.

After pleading our case and finally convincing our vet to see our point, the red X came off. We never let that tech handle him after that. Instead, another male tech handled him more successfully. In fact, he would laugh at Buddy's persistent attempt to commandeer the situation, which made it all the more fun to watch.

It seemed that when Buddy realized you were not going to put up with his games and nonsense, he would

~e. To him, however, he had to at least try to drive
:o the point of insanity. In many instances, he
:eded.

'o effectively deal with Buddy's unflagging
ςy, we made sure to walk him for at least a mile
    day if not more. It did not matter if it was a
beautiful, sunny day with blue skies overhead or
whether it was one of Long Island's greyest and
snowiest of winter days.

Regardless of the weather forecast, Buddy needed
invigorating exercise. This was basically just to keep
us a little sane. Buddy still had unfaltering energy, but
it bought us at least an hour of peace while he was
resting afterwards. During our daily walks we would
run into well-meaning people who would ask the same
question: "Isn't he neutered? I thought neutered dogs
were supposed to be calmer." Yep, we thought the
same thing. Thanks for the educational heads-up.
Obviously, we were dead wrong. We had no
experience with his pre-neutered self to compare to his
post-neutered self, but we can only surmise that it must
have been even crazier.

We encountered other people walking their young
male and neutered and golden retrievers. Their dogs
were calm and obediently walked by their side quiet as
a mouse. Our dog, on the other hand, was pulling,
jumping, barking, and causing a major scene. We
always just assumed that the other dog was older than
ours. When we found out they were the same age, we
realized that we did not have a typical dog on our
hands. Our training techniques couldn't have been that
bad, could they?

During our "getting-acquainted" stage, we learned many things about Buddy. One of the things that we found out was that Buddy was a mischievous and calculating thief. Anything that was within his range on the floor or in jumping distance was not safe. We had to learn to see the world as he saw it, which was low to the ground. This meant getting at his eye level, looking for anything within his line of vision and promptly removing items that he would be more apt to steal.

Unfortunately, we learned this the hard way and a little too late. There were times when his actions were harmless and even funny, and other times when they were a little more disturbing.

One of those times occurred within the first week of owning Buddy before Michael and I were married. Michael called me at my mother's house to say that Buddy had managed to indulge in a tasty bottle cap. It wasn't a nice clean edge soda bottle cap like one would have hoped (if you would hope for such a thing), but a sharp, jagged-edged, metal beer cap. I could not imagine what compelled him to do so, but he had jumped on the counter and thought it was a good idea to chomp down on this. I hope he thought it was worth it as I cannot even imagine the intense pain that he must have endured as he swallowed it.

We felt terrible as we had owned him for less than a week and already this would be our first call to the vet. We awkwardly explained the story to them about how we had just adopted the dog and he was a bit over the top.

In addition, for some reason (most likely due to our nagging guilt) we felt the need to explain that we were not heavy drinkers, but that he just happened to grab the one beer cap from the one bottle of beer that we drank. I'm quite certain that the vet did not particularly care about our drinking habits, but we felt like it was our fault and that we needed to 'fess up.

Once the vet heard our pathetic story, he gave us the following options: get X-rays and operate or wait a few days and see how he was feeling. Since we had never experienced a dog that had dined on rough-edged bottle caps as a snack, we chose to wait a few days. He was not behaving any differently so we assumed that all was okay.

After checking on him constantly and looking for any signs of illness, it turned out that Buddy was fine. We did not think anything of it and almost forgot about it until three weeks later when we found the bottle cap, albeit rusted, on the kitchen floor. There were no surrounding "objects," so we were just thankful we'd found it and made sure to keep anything with sharp edges out of his reach.

We were not sure how it came out...but we decided not to let our imagination get the best of us and just to move on. That information would remain solely between Buddy and the bottle cap.

Unfortunately, it did not end there. The more valuable the item, the more enticing it was for Buddy to steal. My mother reminisces about how she came over to visit one day and mistakenly left her pocketbook open on the bed.

I happened to glance down and saw that it was open and couldn't help but notice Buddy's stuffed animal was inside. I questioned my mother as to why she had his toy in her bag, to which she looked at me like I was losing my mind. In a slight panic, I immediately knew something was up as I couldn't find Buddy and quickly realized that he had been silent for quite some time.

After searching the house, I found him in his crate quietly chewing on something. As I moved in a little closer, he began to wag his tail profusely and bark at me. Whatever he was eating, he tried to devour in a frenzied haste, but could not wolf it down as quickly as he had hoped.

Since he was already in his crate, I had an advantage and was able to grab the remaining object from his mouth without having a full-fledged chase throughout the entire house. What I pulled out of his mouth was a gooey, half-eaten package of cheddar cheese crackers.

That clearly explained the stuffed animal in my mother's purse. My mother just happened to have a small package of cheese crackers in her purse. When we weren't looking, he had ventured into the bedroom, jumped on the bed, looked for a treasure, and stolen his delicious snack. In exchange for the crackers, he placed his toy in there. I suppose he must have thought we would not be smart enough to notice the difference, and, sadly enough, he almost got away with it.

Unfortunately, my niece was a victim of some petty theft from Buddy as well. She, too, had left her purse open while visiting. As was the case when

Buddy was gone for too long, I went looking for him and at the same time, he came running out of the bedroom barking as loud as ever. He had something green wedged between his teeth and was as proud as could be. As we got a bit closer, we saw what it was and couldn't believe that he was at it again.

He had rummaged through my niece's purse, bypassed all of the other items in there, helped himself to her wallet, and selectively pulled out a twenty dollar bill. We were able to salvage it just enough so that it was usable. That is, after we dried the excessive drool off of it.

From that point on, I warned each person that came over with any type of bag to make sure it was tightly sealed and positioned high enough so that Buddy did not have any access to it.

Aside from those two specific burglaries, he frequently stole shoes, sneakers, socks, sunglasses, important papers, pens, plants, and cell phones—anything he was not supposed to have.

When company was brave enough to come over, we gave them fair warning and advised them not to put their belongings anywhere within Buddy's reach. For him, stealing objects that were off limits was much more fun than playing with his own toys.

It did not matter how many different types of toys we bought him, as both his cheap and expensive toys were quickly turning into mere threads inside of a few short days.

To subsidize his toy fetish, I ransacked through the attic of my mom's house to find "puppy-safe" toys I had accumulated during my childhood.

The quicker we provided him with toys, the faster I had to fix them up. I had more stuffed animals in "surgery" than in Buddy's toy chest. I developed some skill at sewing, although I don't think I ever found matching thread. Buddy did not seem to mind. It gave his toys character.

He would obediently wait by my side while I repaired them for him. Ironically, it was one of the few times when he was calm and quiet. I finally figured out why. As soon as I was done, he flashed his beautiful puppy dog eyes, and I would give him his newly renovated toy.

He seemed to like these damaged toys the best; it gave him a challenge to rip it faster and in half the time it had taken me to sew them. Our all-time favorite was one we nicknamed Lobotomy Bunny. Buddy tore off half of its head, which stubbornly I sewed back on. It was quite unattractive to say the least, but Buddy absolutely loved it.

After carrying these around in his mouth for a few days, they became quite dirty. I made sure to wash them every few days, and they were as good as new. I was quickly adapting to the new everyday life of dealing with Buddy.

Since his fetish did not stop at stuffed animals, we realized that we had to keep our sneakers and anything of relevance secured away in the closet. The good thing was that Buddy would not open doors if they were halfway closed. (Well, not unless there was a thunderstorm, which is an entirely different story). This was the one advantage that we had going for us.

We were safe from Buddy getting into something he was not supposed to if we did close the doors halfway, but again this was something we had to gradually learn. More than once we came home to minor disasters, such as our entire house toilet-papered by our beloved dog.

If we did not know any better, this may have startled us at first, but it was easy to identify the culprit. There was no way he could possibly deny this one. Bud's feet had toilet paper stuck all over his pads. As he innocently wagged his tail and barked at us as if to say that we were guilty, his nose had remnants of toilet paper stuck to it as well, as did the jowls of his mouth and his teeth. He was clearly busted; he knew it, and he couldn't have been happier.

Since he found enjoyment in shredding the toilet paper, we had to change where we stored it. Instead of a cabinet, our bathroom sink had a cute curtain-like cover around it where the toilet paper was kept. We removed it from there and hid it out of Buddy's reach, assuming that would take care of any future issues with toilet paper.

This was not the case at all. Buddy learned that he could still get at it while it was on the toilet paper roll in the bathroom. He found an edge he could grab and started pulling. Again, it was all staged for us to come home to his obsession with unsightly redecorating. While funny at first, it became somewhat annoying after a long day at work. The last thing we felt like doing was parading around the house picking up confetti-sized pieces of toilet paper, especially after we'd spent countless hours cleaning the house the previous day.

If that wasn't enough for him, he decided it was enjoyable to go foraging through the trash cans to pick out what was in his eyes a treasure. For the record, there was nothing more disgusting than pulling used and slobbered-on tissues out of the depths of a dog's throat.

Those times were definitely trying. Not really a firm believer in hitting our dogs, our methods of punishment were to give him a "time-out" session in his crate. He grew to recognize the irate tone in our voices so well that if he thought he was in trouble, he would just take the liberty of punishing himself.

He would walk into his crate, glare back at us as if we had some nerve, and occasionally growl at us in what he thought was a threatening way. The amusing thing was that his growl only made us laugh because we knew he was completely incapable of hurting a fly. He had tried to appear mean and vicious by displaying all of his pearly whites as he peeled back his jowls, but we knew better. He wasn't hurting anyone.

When he growled, we would kiss his nose or stick our hands in his mouth just to show him he wasn't fooling anyone though I don't recommend doing this to any dog. He knew we weren't afraid of him one bit. And we knew he was not afraid of us at all. The latter did not exactly work in our favor.

Yelling at him did not faze him. He was never scared of us. In his ongoing quest to steal, he would systematically search for whatever item would get him the most attention. He grabbed whatever he could and instead of hiding the fact that he stole something, he would come find us with his tail wagging out of control and recite what became his trademark stealing bark.

Each time he stole something, he sounded this musical bark alerting us that it was playtime. The more you chased him, the more he would bark, and the faster his tail would wag. It was very difficult to become angry with him while he was clearly having so much fun.

There were times, though, when we grew tired of his actions—for instance when he steal reports for work that we had been diligently working on for hours. He felt that it was good to at least drool on them, or if he was really devoted to giving us a good time, rip them to shreds.

His thievery became such a common routine that we would wait to hear him lugging something up the stairs every morning without fail. One day, it would be a sneaker, another day a shoebox; the next day it would be the sound of him dropping heavy work boots down the stairs, running down to grab it, and trying once more to carry it up. If he finally made it up the stairs, he would jump into bed with us and greet us by dropping the dirty boot on our heads. Getting knocked in the head with a heavy boot was not really a great way to wake up.

He was always up to something and kept us on our toes. One of the funniest memories I have of his puppyhood took place one morning. I awoke to Buddy standing on the floor by the base of the bed with his tail wagging at one hundred miles per hour. As soon as he realized I was awake, his tail moved even faster, like wiper blades on full blast. I could only imagine what this dog had in his possession that would make him this happy. I was a little worried.

As I rose from my peaceful sleep, I patiently awaited the harmonious bark. I could immediately tell if whatever he had was a treasured item from the speed of his tail and the intensity of his bark. This particular bark was about as loud as it gets and his tail could not wag any faster.

As I braced myself for what I was about to discover, there at the base of the bed was Buddy. And there in his mouth was my brand new bra. The straps were stuck between his two front paws as if he was trying to wear it, and apparently, he could not figure out a way to get it off.

If anyone has ever doubted that a dog laughs, trust me. Without a shadow of a doubt, I am positive that they do. I can guarantee this dog found this entire episode to be the funniest thing he had ever experienced up to that point. I chose not to help him since he was so amused; he was loving life and his tail was still wagging away.

I sat and watched for a while, enjoying his determination, but after a few minutes, I had to get up and wrestle with him. He was just too damn cute. He would always win the wrestling match though. He was already way too strong.

To add to Buddy's extra long list of favorite things to steal, scrunchies is probably number one. He has an inexplicable, strong obsession with these things.

Without fail, he can find the scrunchy in any girl's hair and gently but expediently pull it out.

I'd see him actually eyeing my head to see if I was wearing one, or if I was on the floor he would make his move to smell my hair and then make his next move to steal.

Various times I had tried to turn the tables on him and wrap my scrunchy around his snout, but this just made it more entertaining for him. He would always win. He would run off barking and then eventually come back with the scrunchy in his mouth as if to say, "See, you can't outwit me!" He was absolutely right.

There were many mornings when I wore my hair tied up in a scrunchy and foolishly bent down to pick something up, tie my shoe, or get something out of a cabinet. Sure enough, before I could get up in time, there was Buddy ripping the scrunchy out of my hair. It amazed me that he could do so without so much as pulling a hair out of my head.

This pilfering also led to a chase throughout the house: up the stairs, around the dining room table, over the couches, around the coffee table. Anywhere was free game. It was normally entertaining, but when you were late for work or an appointment, it became highly irritating. He did not care one bit. To him, this was considered a great time.

My young niece, who I think was maybe six years old at the time, was utterly terrified of Buddy. She had come over one day for a family party dressed adorably and wearing a bright purple scrunchy in her hair. We were all enjoying the beautiful summer day and eating lunch in the backyard.

I noticed her running and crying with a look of pure terror in her eyes. I did not realize exactly why she was running until she kept screaming that Buddy was trying to eat her head. It took only a second for me to understand. His one desire at that point in time was the bright, enticing scrunchy. He was in the zone, chasing her all over the backyard for this brilliant toy that he assumed was rightfully his. It was at this point that I realized I would never be able to fully explain Buddy's bchavior.

It was situations such as this that kept us laughing and in good spirits. Since the day we brought him home, he had been a hilarious clown. The key to handling Buddy was to be a wise-ass right back. It seemed when we started in with him play-fighting, chasing him, or even dressing him up, he found it to be hysterical.

Some people did not feel the same way, and visits from family and friends were often somewhat stressful depending on the patience threshold of the people visiting. In most of the books that we had read, they explained not to lock up the dog when company came over. This would only make the dog behave worse, associating company with something bad: solitude.

If the person visiting had a love for big dogs, coupled with no fear, he or she stood a chance of surviving the day. That person might only get jumped on once or twice, and maybe a little drool would adhere to his or her clothes.

If the person did not really like dogs, or exhibited any hint of fear, that person did not have a prayer. It was a nightmare for everyone involved, except, of course, for Buddy. He would sense the person's uneasiness from the second he or she walked through the door and make it a point to torture that person for the entire day. He might relax for a little while and then jump up from a seemingly deep sleep, only to focus on that one fearful individual the entire time.

When I say "jump," I do not mean the occasional hop. I mean a full-fledged jump in the person's lap, kiss his or her face, and put his paws on the person's shoulders to try and dominate type of jump. If he or she were carrying anything, Buddy's main goal was to carry it for them. Not such a good idea if the item happened to be a cake or a glass of red wine.

We consistently had to caution people of his peculiar behavior and try to assure them that this dog was not going to hurt them. They rarely believed us and often glared at us with a mixture of apprehension and loathing. The more they backed up to escape this monstrosity, the more Buddy interpreted this as an invite to jump higher and faster. This was another one of the bad habits that he had acquired prior to living with us that we had to break him of.

Some people suggested kneeing him in the chest to make him stop. I did not have the heart to use any blunt force with him. All I kept thinking was that he would get tired eventually—wouldn't he?

Those who were not terrified did not know what to do so they nervously laughed. This only encouraged Buddy more. We were in an awkward position of trying to get people to come over to our house despite Buddy's over-eager hospitality.

Only our dog-loving friends found the experience somewhat enjoyable. For the rest, we really wanted to post a sign instructing on how to act near him:

Please speak to him in a calming voice, and just don't get up quickly. Do not laugh too loud, don't look at him, and don't move around too much. In addition, do not carry your drinks anywhere near him, and do not leave your valuables anywhere that he can see them. If he is misbehaving, turn your back and ignore him (as if this is possible). Do not pet him unless he is sitting, etc.

We never did post that sign, but now that we look back, perhaps it might have helped.

It was important to us to keep him included in our family outings, so one day we decided to bring him to my mother's house for a party. Again, we assumed that after a long walk and a half-hour car ride, he would be tuckered out and would calm down. Wrong. He ran through the house like an unleashed maniac, recklessly exploring all rooms within seconds.

I completely forgot about some of the things in my mother's house and did not doggy-proof it quite as well as I had thought. For example, my mother has little stuffed animals carefully arranged in a decorative sled. Within minutes of us being there, Buddy had dug through the stuffed animals and grabbed two or three of them in his mouth. He then ran top speed again, barking and jumping all over the place and terrorizing everyone there.

He ran downstairs and discovered my two cockatiels in a cage which he promptly jumped on, scattering bird food and feathers all over the place before I could catch up to him. Thankfully, the birds survived it, but Buddy was insistent and kept trying to play with them. I shut the door and locked Buddy out of the birds' room but he kept crying incessantly by the door. After a few more hours of this, we had no choice but to take him home. He was completely obsessed with becoming friends with the birds. I don't think they shared his enthusiasm.

His behavior was similar to that of a problem child whose behavior the parents complain about, but that everyone else finds hysterical. He was methodical in his thinking and had the greatest sense of humor. If you could step back for one moment and move away from the scientific aspect of dogs versus humans, Buddy was the epitome of a stereotypical wise-ass kid. His motive was never to hurt, but to try to make you laugh, play, and well, sometimes to dominate. He could push the most patient person to the point of an explosive temper and then bring them back with his beautiful eyes that exclaimed, "I was just playing!"

Since he'd learned all of these bad behaviors before we adopted him, it grew to the point where we needed to strategically determine his next move before he did. Once we were made privy to his way of thinking, things started to make sense, and on rare occasions we actually won a few of the battles. Slowly, but surely, we were making progress.

With some dogs, it is all about changing the routine each day. With Buddy, we found the exact opposite. Routine helped us in a major way. He ate breakfast the same time each morning and dinner at the same time each night. So that he didn't choke on his food, we fed him half of it, let him eat that, and then gave him the other half, with him waiting for our command of "okay" before starting his meal. A trainer actually asked to borrow that feeding process to use for his obedience class.

To keep with his routine, we took Buddy on a walk five to seven days per week usually after dinner. He knew when we would be coming home each day from work as we would always find him anxiously waiting by the window the moment we pulled in the driveway. On the weekend, his walks took place once, twice, or even three times a day.

Routine helped us to communicate effectively with Buddy as well and understand what he wanted or needed. Though I would never truly want to admit it, we grew to read his body language so well, that we could determine the underlying situation behind some of his most bizarre behavioral patterns. If he was really acting up, to the point that nothing I did calmed him down, that simply meant he had to poop.

When he stood by the bathroom crying, it meant there was an empty toilet paper roll he wanted to play with. While walking up the stairs, if he was walking by our side, pausing on each step while staring at us, he wanted to carry whatever it is that we were holding. If his tail wagged really fast, he had just stolen something of maximum importance and was looking forward to being chased.

He even let us know when he wanted his teeth to be cleaned. He would linger by the bathroom sink and wait for us to get his own toothbrush and chicken-flavored toothpaste. Some dogs won't let you near their teeth. Buddy, on the other hand, was always obsessive about getting his teeth brushed. He had the most perfect white teeth, even in his adult years.

Lastly in the ever-growing list of Buddy's idiosyncrasies, and probably the most important, if Buddy was ever quiet, we knew we had to run and find him…quickly. Whatever he had stolen was so good that he had to relish the moment before he letting you know he stole it.

These are the little, but important things that we learned throughout the past few years of his life…and we were hoping to learn more for a few more years to come.

Knowing these tidbits of information, I had written down some detailed instructions for when the time came for us to travel and go on vacation. Our friends and family laughed when they saw what was involved. When they finally did agree to consider taking care of Buddy in our absence, their faces turned white as I handed them a five-page manual on how to outsmart him.

"Is this really necessary?"

"He is just a dog—how hard can it be?"

Michael and I just looked at each other and knew we were in for it. We were quite certain that we were going to hear of disasters to come.

After I distributed the manual, I did not get any enthusiastic volunteers. Immediately, they all claimed that they had somehow forgotten about a previously scheduled engagement and they were sorry, but they couldn't help.

The few who stepped up to the plate and had the privilege of watching him at various times have been one of Michael's friends and my mother and sister.

My mother, whom Buddy adores, laughs as she tells the story of how Buddy stole her sneakers and then forced her to chase him, only to then steal her ball of yarn a second later while she was crocheting.

Naturally, he had to run around the house like a maniac with that prize. After that debacle, we decided to kennel him while we were away, and thankfully, he and the employees were still in one piece when we picked him up.

We could not, however, manage to get him groomed at a professional dog salon. Every time we tried, it usually started off the same and ended the same. We let the groomer know that Buddy was a little hyper, perhaps more so than most.

Their first response was, "Oh, do not worry about it at all. We groom lots of dogs every week and there are always crazy ones in the mix. He'll be just fine. We have a complete staff that is fully experienced and can easily calm him down."

"Uh, huh. Okay, I'll bring him right in," I'd say, knowing in my heart that it was not going to work out, but secretly hoping that just this one time it would.

Sure enough, more than once, after about an hour of Buddy's arrival at the groomer, we received desperate calls from the main person in charge. I knew what conversation would take place as I noticed the phone number flash on the caller ID.

As I answered, we politely exchanged greetings until the conversation took a turn and sounded a little something like this: "We are so sorry, but we are unable to control Buddy. He keeps barking and almost hung himself on the grooming table. We cannot get him to sit down. There will be no charge, but please come collect him as soon as possible."

Knowing this, we decided it would probably be best for everyone involved if we were to groom him ourselves.

We went out and bought shampoo, a brush, nail clippers, and a doggy-strength razor. It was not the groomers' fault. It took two of us to hold him down just to brush Buddy.

Clipping his nails was something of an all-day task, and shaving him was split up over a period of two days. There were some days when he walked around with half of his body shaved for a day or two, until we got the energy to shave the other side. While he was always clean, sometimes he looked like he had a bit of a rough night.

As the months and years grew on, we grew to know Buddy even better. He was always a challenge to us, but certain things did come together. He was never calm, but activities such as car rides, while never enjoyable, were better.

Buddy learned to stay in the backseat, though not in one spot. He was like a ping pong ball back there, but at least we did not have to wear him as a hat like the first night with him. We tried to get one of those doggy seat belts. This more or less resulted in me wearing the seatbelt and Buddy driving the car. Okay, that might be a slight exaggeration, but let us just say that it did not work out.

We did come to understand that he did not have a bad bone in his body. He was a pure love. The typical hunting instinct that many retrievers possess did not fully find its way into Buddy's character. While he enjoyed hunting for treasures or chasing little creatures, he never wanted to hurt them. I found this out on a whim, but it was interesting to watch. During the first few months of us living with him, I let him outside in the backyard one night as I always did. He took off like a bat out of hell, and at the same time so did another creature.

Some strange animal that I could not identify was in our backyard. As it met Buddy in the center of the yard, I quickly realized exactly what was lurking back there. Those unsightly glaring eyes and long tail could not be mistaken.

There, meeting Buddy face to face was nothing other than a monstrous, red-eyed, creepy-looking opossum. I think I screamed the most blood-curdling, award-winning, horror-movie scream and probably scared Buddy, the opossum, Michael, and about a third of our neighbors as well.

Michael raced down the stairs thinking I was getting murdered. When he saw that I was alive and well, he noticed me by the back door with one foot planted inside of the house and one foot outside. I couldn't decide if I wanted to stay put or go outside to try to split up a possible fight.

I was terrified for a few reasons. One, I did not know if Buddy was going to attack this creature. Two, I did not know if this opossum was going to kill

Buddy, and three, to reiterate, the opossum that close up was just really freaky-looking.

Michael was the brave one and walked out to the center of the yard where the two animals were positioned. Miraculously, the opossum ended up playing possum like he was dead on the ground. Buddy just smelled it, looked at me as if I were a bit strange, and moved on to his potty area.

He left the opossum where it was and kept on walking, not hurting a hair on its unattractive opossum head. The opossum got up and leisurely walked to its original location, wherever that may have been. Neither of them seemed affected by their chance meeting, yet I was the one still trying to recover from a safe distance.

Later that same year, there was an injured bird hobbling around in the backyard. As I let Buddy outside, I had not yet noticed exactly what it was, but I did see something moving awkwardly in the corner of the yard. I realized that it was some kind of wildlife and with regret, thought that Buddy would make that his dinner before I could stop him.

Again, Buddy ran full speed to say hello to this creature, but abruptly stopped short. He soon realized the bird was injured, barked, and ran halfway toward me, barked, and scurried back. He did this a couple of times and then circled around the bird. I hurried over to see what he was up to and soon realized. Buddy seemed relieved to have gotten my attention and assistance. He could have easily killed this bird, but had not touched it. He just did not have the heart to hurt anything.

Though he could be classified as certifiably insane, he was great with all animals, kids, and people. He just had too many owners, bad training, and an overabundance of energy. There was not enough exercise that would keep his abnormal energy level content.

We were able to deal with him and understood that we had a lot of hard work ahead of us to break his habits, but at times it was trying. He was sometimes such a menace, and a lot of times simply out of control.

We did not mind so much that he would do outrageous things, such as jump up and down on the couches, but there was an incident one day that involved breaking one of our matching lamps that we had purchased only a few weeks prior.

After jumping on the couch, he was trying to tackle Michael, and in the midst of his wild episode, he knocked over the ceramic lamp, shattering it into tiny little pieces. We got so annoyed at him because he just would not stop...ever. He always wanted to play-fight. It never ended.

After mulling it over for a while, we started to analyze the situation. We felt badly for him since he was alone all day long with no one to pal around with. It was possible that he was the type of dog that just needed a playmate who could keep up with him.

After some deliberation, we figured we would try to find him one. How could a dog with so much energy be alone all day while we worked? As it turned out the timing was somewhat perfect to invite a new puppy into our lives; however, the circumstances allowing that timing were not.

Chapter 5-A Friend for Buddy

To conquer loneliness, it is nice to have a friend to pal around with, snuggle with, and, of course, start a long-awaited wrestling match with!

It was the day after 9/11 when I got let go from my supposedly stable and decent job at the company where I had been employed for ten months. While watching the events of the terrible attack unfold on a small television in the office, I heard the owner of the company mumble to himself that the towers' falling "wasn't good for business."

I never understood how this person could focus on what was good for business while people were suffering or dying, and the United States had just begun its war on terror.

The next day, he let the newest employees go, which included me since I had been there under a year. The events of 9/11 were devastating enough and this lay-off just added to the eerie and disconsolate silence that existed during that horrible time.

Initially, I was upset about the lay-off, but I placed some phone calls to contacts I had made throughout the years. Luckily, I was able to land another job with an employer from a previous job. I would need to wait approximately two months for a position to be made available for me, though, so I had some time to relax and actually enjoy my time off.

Michael and I agreed it would be a good idea to start visiting the puppy stores since I was unemployed and would have ample time to train a puppy during the day. It was a tough decision since we had not even had Buddy for ten months, but due to the fact that I loved dogs and had plenty of time, I figured we could make it happen.

If we had survived Buddy, we could certainly handle another dog. We searched around and found a few viable possibilities. In one store, they advertised an extremely low price for a golden retriever. We could not wait to meet her, as we assumed it was this cute three-month-old that had been there for a few weeks.

We asked if we could play with her while we waited to speak to someone. Without actually confirming that this pup was the one for sale, we took her into the puppy playpen to get acquainted.

After playing with this pup for a few minutes, another employee came into the little pen and smiled at us curiously, wondering why we were playing with this particular pup.

He then asked us if we were ready to sign the adoption papers. Thankfully, we made sure that one was the correct one for sale.

"Well, we saw the discount price on the window and we would love to take her. She is perfect." I think we already had her name picked out and kept talking amongst ourselves.

He shook his head and politely interrupted. He kind of chuckled, put his hand on his chin, and said, "That is not the one for sale. That one costs full price. Let me get the one that is for sale."

With a slight sense of confusion, we just sort of looked at each other and waited patiently for the inexpensive dog.

After about three minutes, we heard some footsteps coming from the back room, followed by panting, running feet, and rattling chains banging against the side of the wall. In an instant, the employee returned somewhat out of breath, gained his composure, and said, "This is the dog for sale."

There are certain times in a person's life when things just fall into place and start to make sense. This was one of those said times. The price tag on this particular dog was marked down for a very good reason.

We surmised that the impish dog that was brought in panting and carrying on must have been Buddy's younger brother. He was jumping all over the place, barking, stealing toys, and climbing on our laps.

He displayed the same type of insane, ludicrous behavior that we had grown to know all too well.

Michael and I looked at each other, glanced at the disheveled employee, and kindly said, "Thank you, we have changed our mind. We have to go now."

I don't recall who ran out first or whether I pushed Michael or he pushed me, but all I do know is that we immediately ran out of that store as if it had caught on fire. It was that particular episode that forced us to analyze our decision, acknowledging the fact that a new dog could quite conceivably behave just like Buddy.

We joked about that experience later, but I can only hope that the pup got adopted into a loving home, as it was easy to see that he was another sweetheart of a dog. I pray the person who was blessed with him had tons of patience and even more understanding.

A lot of times people buy dogs because they are cute as puppies or they think it would be a nice gift for the kids. They do not take into consideration that these puppies do grow. If not trained properly when they are young, they develop habits that are often difficult to break, as was the case with Buddy.

This can lead to many different avenues, but some of the more common ones are that either the grown dog gets returned because the owners do not know how to handle them or the dog gets abused. Some people are convinced that "tough love" will train the dog.

We just were not capable of trying to train two of the same kind of high-intensity dogs. We knew Buddy would consume most of our time, and we could not have two uncontrollable dogs with bad behavioral issues. We decided to keep looking.

After a few days of searching, we finally narrowed it down to two dogs that we really wanted. We joke that the one I wanted was a boy dog for $255, and the other one that Michael wanted was a girl for $195. Both were adorable, of course. She was a little older (six months) and little less expensive. After some careful deliberation, we decided that both her age and the reasonable price tag were the determining factors that made her "the one."

One thing we both agreed upon was that her name was going to be Brandi with an *i* at the end.

We adopted Brandi on October 6th, 2001. She was exactly six months old and had a little more of a reddish color for her coat. Once again, we had the ride home all planned out. I would sit in the passenger seat while Michael put her on my lap. We were prepared for another night just like the one driving home with Buddy.

Michael started the car, and we waited. Brandi just sat there as calm as could be with her front paws crossed over one another like a proper lady. She did not move the entire time. If this was to be a clear indication of how perfect she would become, someone must have been watching over us. She was the exact opposite of Buddy.

We could not wait to bring her home. Buddy would be so happy to have a playmate that could keep up with him. It would be awesome. We figured this would totally subdue Buddy if he had someone to romp around with all day. We drove home trying to remain calm, anticipating Buddy's ecstatic reaction…or so we thought.

As it turned out, Buddy was not ecstatic. He was not even remotely amused. He looked about as happy as someone who'd just been fatally stung by a swarm of bees. If I ever thought a dog could curse me out, it was at that precise moment.

Even though they had bathed her at the shop, she did not have that adorable, sought-after new puppy smell. Instead, Brandi had a very undesirable and distinct odor to her. We thought it was just from the puppy store, and we would bathe her again when we got home. She was twenty-nine pounds, so we were able to easily place her in the sink to wash her. Well, Buddy smelled it, too. As soon as he saw her, his face said it all. He looked at us with disdain, and then we noticed that he was foaming at the mouth. Not in the rabid sense, but foaming nonetheless.

Brandi, still sporting the crazy, big, ridiculous bow from the puppy store, was thrilled to meet him and began lavishing him with puppy kisses and jumping on him with pure delight. Buddy quickly walked into the other room, disgusted. As much as Brandi wanted to play with him, he gave her the cold shoulder and walked away.

Here was precisely when we learned that when Buddy was upset he actually moped in the full dramatic sense of the word: head hanging low, feet dragging, and eyes drooping. He even occasionally threw in a heavy, exasperated sigh for added effect.

We found out after three more baths and an initial trip to the vet that the putrid smell was none other than disgusting ear mites. It was the most repulsive and unforgettable stench. The vet informed us that this was most likely the reason that Buddy frothed at the mouth. We immediately picked up some medicine for the mites, and we had to sanitize anything that Brandi had been near. This included washing all linens, cleaning the crates, and vacuuming the carpets…again.

We also discovered that we must have signed up for the bonus package as Brandi had left the pet store with worms, no extra charge. Unfortunately, we found this out while we were eating our dinner—not something you really want to discuss. Again, we acquired some more medicine for this, and she was as good as new. Buddy, on the other hand, was still adjusting to the fact that he was no longer the only dog, but when he wasn't looking we did catch him studying Brandi with intense curiosity.

The first few days we suffered from buyer's remorse. Since the initial problems with the ear mites and worms, we were no longer sure that a second dog was such a smart move. After all, there was so much work involved with training Buddy, and a second dog would be double the work.

We hadn't even thought about the extra expense that a second dog would bring us.

Through a few discussions and some tears, we needed to take a break to get our thoughts together. Michael locked Brandi in her crate while he took a long-needed nap, and I ran to the store to clear my head and get out for a while.

When I came home, Brandi's crate was still locked; however, she was sitting outside of it just looking at me. I surmised that Michael had lost his mind and forgotten to put Brandi in her crate before he locked it. I put her back in her crate, locked it, and went to wake Michael.

When I woke him, I gently asked him if he'd forgotten to put Brandi in the crate. He looked at me like I was insane, and I told him where she was when I came home. We went back downstairs and sure enough, there she was sitting outside of her crate again, with the door still locked. We nicknamed her Houdini, since we don't really know how she got out, but she never did it again after that.

After the initial shock of owning two dogs, we were still deciding if we should keep her. Michael decided to have a private talk with Brandi by our backyard tree discussing the rules of the house. We often declared later that she understood, because she was nearly perfect after that day, and, yes, we did keep her.

A few days later, Buddy determined that it was time for him to show Brandi who was the boss and the king of the house. Even though he was neutered, he decided to meander to where Brandi was sitting and mount her time and time again. Again, through our research, we found out this was not a sexual thing but more about dominance. He was trying to show Brandi he was in charge. Brandi was fine with this for the most part. She was well adjusted and did not feel the need to compete.

Things went on like that for a while until Buddy pushed her to the point of intense frustration. He was playing and playing and enticing her to play a little more. She was growing kind of tired of this and just wanted to have some downtime.

Buddy obstinately pressed on as he always did. This time, however, Brandi decided to teach him a valuable lesson. She grabbed onto his ear and held on tight. She held on with so much force that Buddy screamed in pain, but Brandi refused to relent. I yelled at her and yelled some more, but she wouldn't let go.

Finally, though I am not proud of this, I threw my cell phone down in an attempt to scare her with the loud noise, and it accidentally bounced and hit her. It did not hit her hard, but it was enough to make me feel guilty and get her off of Buddy. After that, I put her in her crate and made some loud noise to kind of scare her, and she never bit him like that again. Luckily, she had been gentle enough not to draw any blood. She did succeed in teaching Buddy a lesson, too. She had become the new Alpha dog.

We were well on our way to having one very obedient dog and another that still would not calm down. Despite their initial meeting, these two dogs quickly grew fond of each other. Brandi looked up to Buddy, and Buddy secretly loved his new playmate. They would play all day and look out for each other. It was beautiful to watch. After the one episode of the ear biting, they never hurt each other. Not once. They would play, nip, growl, and enjoy every minute of it. Brandi would entice Buddy to play by stealing his toys, and Buddy would always take the bait.

When she wanted to, Brandi intimidated Buddy by standing over him and staring intensely as he gnawed on his Nyla-Bones. Eventually, Buddy would give it up and Brandi would take over. The same behavior took place when they were at the water bowl. Buddy could be extremely parched with thirst, but when Brandi came over he would allow her to have first dibs, patiently waiting until she finished. He was genuinely a sweetheart. This was all done on his own. I wish we could take the credit, but we never once taught him manners. That was one thing he most likely picked up from his biological mom.

Not everything was perfect. We did encounter some minor issues with Brandi. Since we were learning as we went along, it took us about a year before Brandi was fully housebroken. We did not have any previous experience housebreaking a dog, so we were practicing all of the wrong techniques. Allowing her to roam freely in the fully carpeted living room after she drank a bowl of water may not have been on our list of the smartest things we ever did.

Soon after, we learned what to do and what not to do. For instance, we did not feed her before bedtime, and we removed her water bowl a couple of hours before going to sleep. We also made sure she urinated a few times prior to bedtime. In addition, it was important to divide the crate into two sections, giving her only enough room to turn around, increasing her living space as she got older.

This last piece of advice was a funny one because we did not have a real divider, so we used a piece of wood that sectioned off the entire width of the crate, but not so much the height. Brandi realized she could jump into the second section to take care of business and then back into the clean side for the remainder of the night.

That was another lesson we learned and promptly resolved. We bought a real crate divider that actually extended both the full width and height of the crate. We were slowly learning.

Other than those small issues, she was very well behaved. Shy amongst strangers, she would literally climb to the back of her crate upon meeting new people, but once comfortable, she would come out and be happy to socialize.

Typically, she never chewed anything other than her toys, which she instinctively knew were hers to play with. We thought she was perfect, and for the most part she was. That is, if you didn't consider coming home to a half-eaten couch a bad thing.

It happened one day after a particularly rough afternoon at the office. I came home at the same time that I normally did. Once I walked inside of the house, I immediately noticed what had transpired during the day. I knew it was not Buddy because he had never been destructive. Crazy, yes. Destructive, no. Brandi had the word "guilty" written all over her puppy-dog face. My dilemma was split between what to deal with first, correcting Brandi or how to grudgingly tell Michael.

Since Brandi was in front of me at that precise moment, I decided to deal with Brandi first. Correcting her was a tough one.

Most of the training manuals had said that you cannot successfully reprimand a dog unless they were caught in the act. Otherwise, they genuinely had no idea why you were correcting them. They lived in the moment, and something they'd done five minutes before was long forgotten and obsolete in a dog's mind. Brandi got off on a technicality for that one.

I tried to at least point and say no but she looked at me with a sweet expression on her face and just blinked. I knew my correction technique was not working, as I came home the next day and I had matching couches. I finally smartened up and purchased Bitter Apple spray, which was to deter dogs from chewing or licking any objects that they should not chew, including furniture. Thankfully, it never happened again.

Surprisingly, when I told Michael the news, he handled it quite well. It was an old couch, and we were about ready for a new one. Thank goodness for small favors. I was glad we hadn't purchased a new couch prior to adopting Brandi.

Raising two dogs was not without its rewards and we were doing the necessary things to make their life a pleasant one. Within a few weeks of her adoption, it was time to get Brandi spayed. We decided that I would stay at my mom's with Brandi during her recovery period because Buddy was just too hyper. We did not want him accidentally ripping any of her stitches by playing too rough. She was perfect at my mom's and did not have any accidents. She did not even pay any attention to the cockatiels.

While we were staying there, I had made a decision to give the cockatiels away to a better home (though I feel badly now for doing so). I felt they were not getting enough attention and that they would do better elsewhere, ironically similar to Buddy's story with his previous owners. During that same time, we thought Buddy and Brandi were missing each other, so Michael brought Buddy over to visit.

Buddy was happy to see Brandi, but after their initial greeting, he ran directly downstairs to where the cockatiels had been. When he did not see them, he started whimpering and carrying on. He peeked behind the door where they once were, circled outside the room, smelled the floor, and then returned back to the location where the original bird cage was.

He then looked at me with the saddest face imaginable, giving me the worst type of guilt trip before moping away. It was at that moment that I realized two important things. First of all, I felt terrible for giving away the birds, and Buddy had magnified that feeling of guilt for me by searching for them. Secondly, Buddy (and probably most dogs) did not forget. It had been months since he had seen those birds, and yet he remembered them and their exact location.

After the two-week recovery period for Brandi, we were finally able to bring her home again. Thankfully, she was back to her old self and seemed happy to be where she was most comfortable.

She was turning out to be a very easy dog compared to Buddy. If I were to write a book about Brandi, it would be very short and sweet. She just listened to the commands as they were given without giving us any heartache. Buddy, on the other hand, actually thought about the commands, determining whether or not they fit with his current mood and then deciding if he is going to follow through or not. I swear that you could actually see him deliberating the outcome of his actions.

He knew what would get him in trouble and then took the time to contemplate whether it was worth it or not. A prime example of this took place after one of our evening walks around the block. We always walked the dogs with a leash, but whenever we got close to our front door, we took them off of the leash to let them run home. We never had issues with this routine. Well, one night we followed the same routine and were not really paying much attention, but there waiting for us on our doorstep was our neighbor's skittish cat. We knew that Bud would never harm a cat, but a chase is a chase and he was certainly up for the challenge.

It did not matter that we had just walked for two miles and that we were exhausted. Buddy still had tons of energy and he took off like a speed demon, crossing our extremely busy street and running in the dark away from our house. I did not know where I learned all of the obscenities I screamed, but they were coming out of my mouth full-force. I could have sworn Buddy was definitely going to get hit by a car that night.

My heart was racing. I had to make a quick decision whether to run after him or go inside of the house, get the keys, and drive to find him. As mad as I was, I was devastatingly upset. Not that we could have foreseen a cat lounging by our front door, but that we should have known better than to let a hyperactive, insane pup off of the leash in the front yard.

As I proceeded to go into the house and grab my car keys, out of nowhere a flash of fur came running toward me. My sadness and worry quickly transformed into anger once again, and I started screaming at him. Since I had never previously raised my voice at this dog, he immediately knew he was in deep trouble.

He ran straight past me, through the open door, past the living room, into the kitchen, and way back into the corner of his crate. I did not have to say a word. He knew he had made a bad decision, but his instinct and desire to chase had outgrown his fear of how much trouble he would get in.

Brandi was calm as could be while she watched the entire scene unfold. At first she had attempted to follow him, but promptly came to us when we called her. She had always been the ultimate perfect angel. If every dog were destined to behave like Brandi, I could guarantee that we would own about five or six if not more.

This was just one of many nights that were stressful as we tried to contain Buddy. Admittedly, I did not have tons of patience with certain people, but I had the utmost patience and tolerance when it came to dogs. Put me in a room with ten people and I would be annoyed in five minutes. Put me in a room with ten friendly dogs and I would be in my glory.

Buddy, however, continually tested us to the fullest of his ability. Even I was at my breaking point. I could not think of enough ways to outmaneuver him. Any time we thought we had his tactics all figured out, he would learn our tricks and then outsmart us again. Growing up, we had many dogs, but none even came close to having Buddy's idiosyncrasies, and none of them behaved as badly. I did not know how we were going to handle both.

Chapter 6-Training

While observing some people with their dogs, it is often a question of who is training whom. It is not uncommon to see an owner with their arms extended, holding on for dear life, while their dog runs wild. Unfortunately, I was becoming one of those owners.

Moving forward, training Brandi was something of a chore. This was not because Brandi was bad, but because Buddy, although mischievous, was an extremely smart dog. During our sessions, I tried to teach Brandi to sit and had my training treats handy. Buddy would join in and sit on command.

When I tried to ignore him and focus solely on Brandi, he growled, moved a little closer, and sat again. I could see the wheels spinning in his mind, saying, "I am sitting. Give me a treat!"

He was doing exactly what I had asked only I was not asking him. Brandi would then expect a treat as well and simply could not or would not concentrate until I gave her one. This went on for days. I tried to lock Buddy in a separate room, but then Brandi just focused and obsessed upon looking for her best pal, Buddy.

Buddy was no help as he would yelp and bark from the other room, causing Brandi to continuously search for him until I let him out.

It got to the point where I actually opened up a beer at twelve o'clock in the afternoon. I had never had much of a drinking problem, but you might have thought differently when Michael called me from work to see how things were going. I answered the phone with a slight slur in my voice telling him that all was going well. My technique, however, did work.

From that day forward, I developed a bit more patience and was actually able to find training enjoyable. Of course, beer was no longer necessary. Brandi actually learned to sit, lie down, roll over, and give her paw. She easily mastered the commands for "come" and "stay."

The one trademark move Buddy could not handle her doing was his high five. Whenever I tried to teach her that, he would move closer to me, growl, and offer me his high five, first his left paw, then his right. He would also make an attempt to block me from teaching Brandi.

I let him keep that as his own personal trick since that was the first one I had ever taught him. He never appreciated when another dog would do it. Any time I would ask another dog for a high five he would growl, come closer to me, and give me a high five. That one was his.

The two dogs became inseparable and actually began to look forward to training. If I brought out a cookie, they would immediately sit, give a high five/give a paw, beg, lie down, crawl, and then roll over. I did not even have to issue the commands anymore. They just did it automatically. Training became fun for all of us.

Once we got the important commands down, Michael and I were able to teach them little tricks here and there. Michael taught Buddy the popular trick of guessing which hand the cookie was in. He always figured it out on the first try. Brandi, not so much. It took her a few attempts. She was beautiful but not as smart as Buddy, which was most likely the reason why she was so well-behaved and easy to train.

As for Buddy, when I say I literally had "blood, sweat and tears" during our beginning training sessions, I truly did. His mouthing, while playful, was extremely painful, as he did have strong, adult teeth. It sometimes left me with bruises, and occasionally he even broke the skin. He was playing the entire time, but he did not realize his own super strength.

It was tough to break this awful pattern, since his previous owners had handled this by letting him gnaw on a bone as a way to remove his mouth from their arm. Buddy continued this habit, thinking that he would get a treat and did not comprehend that he was actually doing something bad.

I've heard some people say to shove a fist down a dog's throat to stop him, while others advised us to bite Buddy back. We chose not to do either, but we did take one word of advice which was to shrilly cry "ouch" as he bit down.

This suggestion seemed to have worked the best as he soon understood that he should not bite all the way down, and he learned to mouth in a gentle way. He never bit down again after a few sessions of this technique.

Michael would tickle Buddy's tongue if Buddy went to mouth him too hard. This, as funny as it sounds, worked like a charm.

I had never realized that there were so many different tactics to learn about training a dog. Basically, any dogs that I had previously owned while living at my mother's house were taught to sit, come, and stay, and that was the extent of the training. We never had any issues like the ones we were experiencing with Buddy.

With Buddy, we had to think way out of the box if we were going to make it work.

Each aspect of training had to be carefully planned out, and we always needed to overcome new obstacles with this dog. While that sounds easy, it was probably one of the most exerting things we had to accomplish, both physically and mentally.

Even walking him was a strenuous activity as he was incredibly strong and pulled like a tempestuous beast. Amongst the items that were given to us in our "Buddy care package" was one of those medieval choker collars. It may sound inhumane, but we had no clue how to deal with his behavior. We put the collar on him, and it seemed to facilitate his walks. Even though he still pulled a lot, he was a little bit more manageable.

While walking one morning, we met our neighbor for the first time, who smiled as he noticed our obvious struggle with Buddy.

He walked over, introduced himself, and simply said "May I?" before grabbing hold of the leash. He whispered a few words to Buddy, and we could have sworn that Buddy was an award-winning show dog, and that he and our neighbor were long-lost pals.

Our neighbor even wondered if he had met this dog before. Buddy strolled calmly, right by his side, and did not pull one bit. It was amazing. We were in disbelief as we had been struggling for months to get this dog to listen, and it took our neighbor all of five minutes.

"So, how did you do that?" In the months that we had owned Buddy, we had never been able to keep him five feet in front of us, much less by our side. To make us feel a little bit better, it turned out our neighbor was a dog trainer. He demonstrated once again, explained what he'd done, and then handed me the leash. I finally felt confident that I could control this dog. It was all so simple.

As fast as that thought had entered my mind was as fast as that thought subsided. Somehow, I don't think I appeared quite as graceful. As I stood up straight, I grabbed the leash and began my walk with Buddy. I tried mirroring my neighbor's walking technique, but Buddy pulled me without any effort.

He pulled so much that within one minute my sneaker flew off of one foot, and I was chasing him down the road with one sneaker on and one sneaker off. I had both hands on the leash, trying to gain some type of dignity and composure. I'm sure it was quite a comedy act for anyone watching.

I did not find it so funny, as my face was blushing with embarrassment and my hands were raw from the crazy dog pulling me. I would not dare show my hands. I felt like a complete failure and knew that Buddy was just laughing in the only way that dogs could.

While I mumbled curses under my breath, Michael and our neighbor kind of chuckled. Our new friend proceeded to talk us out of the good old choker collar and turned us on to the harness instead. This was like a skit from a magic show to put on, but it yielded great results. I think Buddy knew how to put the thing on better than we did.

To our pleasant surprise, Buddy pulled much less. We learned to hold the leash midway to keep him closer, loosening the leash when he was being good. We tried to make him focus on us instead of us focusing on him.

The leash actually served as an extension of my arm, so if I was tense, the dog would sense that by the tension of my grip on the leash. Ideally, according to my neighbor, we wanted to be able to be in command of the dog while there is still plenty of slack in the leash.

Since our neighbor was a trainer, he was very resourceful and recommended some helpful strategies. We told him about our desperate attempts to be in command of Buddy. He explained that we should not mix two commands, such as "Sit down!" "Sit" means sit, and "down" means lie down. When we mixed the two, the dog would get confused as if to say, "What is it that you want?"

We were also advised to change the tone of our voice and speak clearly when we were issuing a command, so it would get Buddy's attention and he would know that what we were saying was important. Well, with this, our voice somehow sounded like the beginning of the Black Sabbath song "Ironman." All that did was send Michael and me into a fit of hysterical laughter while Buddy cocked his head at us as if to say, "Idiots," and kept on doing his thing.

We learned that yelling at any dog was not going to yield the desired results. For a dog to obey their master they needed to trust that the master was sane enough to give the precise commands. No amount of yelling was going to portray that type of leadership. All it did was depict instability. It may have caused them to fear their owner, but they would not recognize you as the Alpha dog.

If a dog was going to listen, they would obey a quiet voice. No yelling or screaming was necessary. It was all starting to make sense.

We were lucky in one particular aspect, as despite all of his issues, Buddy demonstrated quite impressive etiquette. During our walks he never stopped to relieve himself on someone's property or in the middle of the street. He always waited until we were near a vacant area to take care of business.

In addition, as bad as he was during these early years, he managed to practice great table manners. He would lie down without crying, begging, or jumping while we were eating our meal. We decided to give him table scraps if and only if he was good. It was the one thing that worked out to our favor. Nine times out of ten, he learned to behave at dinner knowing he would soon be rewarded with a treat. Brandi caught onto to this, too. They never made a peep. Even at their food bowl, we trained them to both sit and wait until we gave the command of "okay." Then they could eat.

Buddy was always the little gentleman at dinnertime; he actually waited until Brandi had food in her dish before he would begin his meal. We never even had to tell him to "wait." He just did it on his own.

If both of them were exceptionally good, not only would they get table scraps but they would also get rewarded with one of their favorite treats. For Buddy, it was one of the following: carrots, peanut butter, Chinese fortune cookies, or cheese. For Brandi, it was mostly bananas or a small taste of coffee. Although coffee is not good for dogs, we always let her sip a very small drop or two. She would stare us down if we did not.

While things were definitely not easy by any means, we were starting to understand what strategies worked or what tactics merely wasted time. His bad habits were slowly disappearing.

Chapter 7-Comfort Level

As with most relationships, after a few years, you reach a certain comfort level. With humans, you start to read each other's moods better and finish each other's sentences. With dogs, you find out how to resolve issues and turn unreleased energy into a positive and happy experience.

As the years progressed, we grew more attached to Buddy and him to us. We learned how to live with this crazy dog at least on some sort of comfort level. We discovered a schoolyard with acres of land and set him free to run there at least two to three times per week. It was remarkable to observe how fast and how far this dog would go. There was no limit to his energy.

Things did not always go so smoothly if there were people on the field, as dogs were not allowed, and people would get annoyed. It worked for us most of the time, however, and when we took him home, he would rest for a little while and then be ready to go all over again within an hour.

Even during inclement weather, we faithfully adhered to his exerting exercise routine. We had a particularly huge snowstorm one year and took him to the schoolyard afterwards so that he could sprint through the snow. As soon as we let him off of the leash, he hurdled over the super large snow banks with minimal effort and crossed to the other end of the field within mere seconds.

I do not think that we had climbed on top of the first snow bank when he started racing toward us and back again. He was able to run through all of this snow at top speed, while we were struggling to walk five feet.

During the hotter months, we found other ways to keep them occupied and active. Summers were becoming extraordinarily fun. We had an above-ground pool, and our two dogs absolutely loved to swim. Michael bought a gigantic plastic ladder that had steps wide enough so that the dogs could climb in and out of the pool at their leisure while we were present.

Above-ground pools have liners that rip easily, so we had to take caution that the dogs did not get close to it. This was not as simple as it sounds as they would swim toward the deck and frantically try to claw their way out when they were ready.

Again, routine here was the key ingredient to making any of this enjoyable. The days of swimming by ourselves were gone, as the minute we had changed into our bathing suits, the dogs would become wild with anticipation. We usually found them pacing by the outside door waiting to go for a swim.

The ocean was another story as it was a bit easier for them to swim. Since they were able to feel the sand underneath their feet, they would only swim until they could no longer feel it.

In the pool, that was not the case. They knew how to swim just fine, but would come directly to us and latch onto us. We needed to wear t-shirts in the pool to prevent the monstrous scratches they would put on us if we did not.

To give them something to grip, we decided to get them Nerf rafts. This worked out rather well, but I'm sure you've heard about dogs controlling their owners? The rafts took that to the next level. Both of our dogs would lounge on these with expectations for us to pull them around. I half expected them to order a frozen, tropical drink topped with a mini umbrella.

Brandi was more of a passionate swimmer as she would swim from one raft to Buddy's raft just to be next to him—or just to intimidate him, depending upon her mood.

They became completely overjoyed and hyper with excitement each time they got the opportunity to go into the pool. Although we complained as if it were a nuisance, truthfully we had a great time and loved every minute of it.

Without fail, each time they would exit the pool, Buddy, full of adrenaline, would do approximately ten laps around the pool and then run to the "bathroom pen" to take care of business. Brandi would skip the laps and run straight to the pen to do the same. Not once did they ever go to the bathroom in the pool. It was safe to say we were relieved about that.

It became moderately funny when we had visitors over. They would be relaxing in the tepid water, blanketed by the warmth of the hot summer sun, when out of nowhere, two huge masses of fur would jump in the pool and splash them. Some people laughed and others may have grimaced. I don't think we ever invited those who grimaced over again. After all, it was our pups' house, too.

There were some days when we wanted to experience the salty air of the beach. On Long Island, however, there were not many public beaches that allowed dogs. While we knew that they were not allowed, we simply could not resist. How could you have a golden retriever (or two) and not let them swim in the ocean? That was one of my major gripes with Long Island. As big as it was, there were no real dog-friendly beaches or parks for that matter. To us, however, it was well worth the risk. We had to go and venture to the ocean with the dogs.

We decided quite a few times that we would risk it and were going to take our chances. The reward was just too great. We piled everyone into our van and meandered on down to the beach. We always had an incredible time.

As soon as the pups smelled the saltwater in the air, they would become a bit uncontrollable, complete with whimpering and/or barking. This would temporarily grate on our nerves until we arrived at our destination.

Seconds later, when it was time to get out of the van, they were overcome with excitement. They could hardly contain themselves. It was always such a great pleasure to watch them just be dogs. Before we even slid open the door to the van, they were jumping and wagging their tails. We had to stop them from hanging themselves with their leash. All this excitement—just to go swimming.

Typically, even though the air could be hot and humid on Long Island, the beach water did not really heat up until August. Prior to August, it was somewhat cold; however, the pups never seemed to mind. In fact, they absolutely loved it.

The first time they went in the water, we tried to put on one of those doggy life preservers. Similar to the seatbelt, it just did not work. The extra-large size was not large enough. Buddy and Brandi were not overweight by any means, but they would not fit.

We had to implement the next best thing. We bought fifteen-foot leads and allowed them to venture out into the water. If they drifted too far and it did not seem like they were coming back anytime soon, we would gently pull on the lead to guide them back toward our direction.

Once or twice, Michael had to go swimming in the ice-cold water when it seemed like the dogs were not listening to us. Secretly, I thought it was a hoax to see if they could get Michael to swim in that water. In all seriousness, I believed Buddy would have swum to Connecticut if he could. He was having that much fun and Brandi was thrilled as well.

At one point, we met another couple who had their golden retriever with them. Their dog was somewhat afraid of the water until he watched ours fearlessly go in. He followed them right in and frolicked with them for a while. Buddy and Brandi accepted him immediately as one of their own. Our dogs always had a way of getting along with other dogs instantaneously as if they had known them their whole lives.

We continued raising them with me living at my mother's house, and then soon after we adopted Brandi, Michael and I got married. We were engaged in May of 2002 and tied the knot in January of 2003. This made it a bit easier to train the dogs now that there were two of us living there...or so we thought.

Brandi never caused any issues. Aside from her initial feast consisting of furniture á la carte, she was truly the most well-behaved dog I had ever encountered.

Although we did use a leash on her, it was never needed. The only time that she ventured off would be to herd Buddy back to us, but other than that, she remained by our side at all times.

She never whined or barked unless approached by another person who had a dog, but after she got to meet the dog, she was fine. This dog was completely content doing whatever it was that we were doing without any complaints. We joked that she was the only mentally stable one in our family.

Buddy continued to be a lot of work. We grew used to it, and we would not want to change a thing. As odd as it sounds, Buddy's antics often sent us into fits of uncontrollable laughter. We wondered what this dog was thinking but could not always figure out the depths of his insanity. As mad as we could get at him, he usually changed our mood rather quickly when we realized all he really wanted to do was play.

He loved having us around to take part in his world, and we grew to feel the same about having him in ours.

There were only a few certain instances when our tolerance level was tested so severely that we could not even think straight. Our next major life decision was one of those disastrous times.

Chapter 8-Road Trip

There are always stressors that can turn a normally peaceful and happy person into a stark raving mad lunatic. Everyone has a breaking point—even if it is subconsciously concealed!

A few years after we were married, we made a major life decision to pack up our belongings and move to Las Vegas, Nevada. We were not thrilled with our neighborhood in New York, and the weather in Las Vegas was unbeatable. There was something to be said for over three hundred days a year filled with beautiful weather and clear blue skies.

We had purchased a summer home there the previous year, and we decided that it would be a great starter house in Las Vegas until we were able to look for another.

It was a charming two-story, two-bedroom house with a loft and tiny balcony overlooking the quiet street. It also had a small but attractive backyard. Land for houses in Las Vegas differed vastly from the land allotments in New York. While yards in Long Island rarely were less than a half-acre, Las Vegas land was measured in feet. We literally had about five feet of backyard from the back of the house to the brick wall that was known as a fence—and we paid a premium to get that. It was adorable, though, and served its purpose for us to get there.

We put our house on the market in November of 2005, and, thankfully, it sold by December. In New York, closing on a house took about three months, so we closed in March 2006, and began our journey across the country that same day.

Knowing Buddy for as long as we had, we already predicted that he was not going to be easy on this trip, so we were mindfully prepared. We had chosen to put both of the pups in dog crates for the long journey. In the event that we ever had to stop short, we wanted to ensure that they would not go flying through the windshield. Buddy was usually content while in his crate and lay down comfortably without complaining. It served as a comfort zone for him. It was the same crate that he'd had since we adopted him and he loved it.

We also brought Benadryl which was supposed to serve as a calming aid to Buddy. (I would not ever suggest you use this for your dog without the advice of your dog's veterinarian.)

Needless to say, none of this worked. After about a half hour into our trip, Buddy decided to chime in with our conversation with some annoying, incessant, loud and infuriating barking.

The drive through New York City alone was stressful without dogs to contend with, as there was an abundance of traffic, too many bridges, and a lot of bad, angry drivers. Adding Buddy to the mix did not help ease the driving situation at all and was a recipe for disaster.

We lasted about three hours and decided to stop in Pennsylvania for the night. It was a long day due to the closing of the house, and we were ready to catch some quality sleep. We were sure that we would be in better moods the next day and that after a long walk Buddy would be fine.

Waking up the next day in Pennsylvania to treacherous ice storms was not something that we counted on and did not add any enjoyment to the trip. Every surface was super slick and dangerously slippery; we could not even find safety on the grass as it, too, was a solid sheet of ice.

I was ready to throw in the towel and suggested to Michael that we should just take the day off from driving, even though it was our first full day.

I despise driving through any type of inclement weather, especially ice or snow, and I felt it was just too dangerous. Michael agreed for about ten minutes and then quickly changed his mind. He wanted to rough out the storm.

Not being much of a daredevil, I put up a small debate and then hesitantly agreed. I wanted to get this long drive over with as well. I figured since we could not take Buddy for that preplanned long walk, we would just administer his first dose of Benadryl the moment he acted up.

I wish I could say that the vet's advice worked for us and that the little pink pills were the ultimate answer to our prayers. This, unfortunately, was not true by any stretch of the imagination. Buddy did not falter; instead, he graced us with his presence by barking the entire time. That was not an exaggeration, not one bit. You would think that no one could possibly carry on for hours on end. Think again.

He barked in octaves I did not even know he possessed. We fed him Benadryl like it was dog biscuits—well, only the recommended amount by our vet, but he still was inconsolable and definitely insane. His crying led to screaming, and his screaming led to barking, and then back to crying again. His voice grew so hoarse we almost did not mind because it was a lower sounding bark, but then he gained his voice right back again.

It got to the point where Michael and I could not hold any conversation at all. If we started talking, Buddy would bark. If we whispered, Buddy would bark. We had no choice but to stop every two hours or any time we saw an open field to let him and Brandi out so that Buddy could run and use up some of his pent-up energy.

Make no mistake, the thought had somewhat crossed our mind to leave him there. His run would buy us about an hour of peace as Buddy would sleep thereafter but once he woke up, he would be right back where he left off, barking and carrying on.

I remember speaking with someone who said golden retrievers were like two-year-old children but that they mellowed out at age three or so. Well, Buddy was six years old when we took this trip and he had not mellowed out at all. I wish I could find that person and tell them how dead wrong they were.

Michael and I were trying our best to keep our calm composure, but we were very rapidly losing it. We were out of intelligent ideas and completely stressed. As we got closer to Vegas, driving up mountains at seventy-five miles per hour with a barking dog was not a good position to be in. I do not know how we did it and lived to tell about it. Four days seemed like an eternity.

While this trip was definitely not enjoyable by any means, there were, in fact, one or two precious moments along the way, mostly once we settled down for the night.

During our travels, we stayed at dog-friendly motels every night to catch up on some sleep. Some were better than others, and some definitely should not have been in business. We were not too picky as we just wanted to catch some shut-eye. That was our main goal.

One evening, we stopped at a hotel that was fairly pleasant and allowed dogs. Inside was a community television room. We ventured across the street for some ice cream, came back, and sat inside this room with our dogs next to us on the couches. It was rather adorable as Buddy and Brandi loved to snuggle.

Without fail, Buddy would bark at people and wag his tail as they walked into his living room. No one seemed to mind as they came over to say hello to him. It was one feeling of normalcy along the way and it calmed all of us down a bit. Buddy was the social butterfly and loved to greet each individual person.

That same night as we were trying to sleep, Buddy kept barking at the ice machine. Though it kept us up for a while, it was hilarious listening to Buddy mutter what he thought were his ferocious growls every few minutes. I think he finally understood after about an hour that the noisy ice machine was not intimated by his growling and barking and we were finally able to get some sleep to prepare for the rest of our road trip.

Chapter 9-Drinks!

Some may call you crazy if you try to reason with a dog. It is with desperate attempts that you hope they understand you. When the realization sinks in that your futile pleading goes without understanding or care, you are left with no choice but to think of the next best thing.

By the time we reached Arizona, day three into our trip, we finally lost it. Full-fledged, certifiably insane lost it. Tempers were flying high, and Buddy's cute face was not cutting it for us. He no longer was that lovable pup. He was now the epitome of evil.

Thoughts of leaving him on the side of the road really seemed like a fantastic and sane idea. No pain reliever was strong enough to get rid of the blaring headaches that felt like a ton of bricks smashing on top of our heads.

It was pure hell, and we were stuck living in it. The whole idea seemed ludicrous, and we thoroughly regretted not throwing the dogs in cargo on a plane regardless of how scared they would be. His five hours of suffering would have been nothing compared to the past three days of dealing with his nonsense.

By nightfall, we had been on the road for about thirteen hours, so we needed to stop for the day. We found another motel that allowed dogs as, thankfully, they were not too hard to come across.

At this point, we were like zombies, not fully awake and mumbling gibberish to each other. We were starving, so we gladly left the dogs in our motel room and walked to Denny's (a popular restaurant typically known for serving breakfast) across the street. We did not say a word and did not really know what to say.

We had only one more day and yet we had no idea how we were going to get through it. Brandi had been an angel the entire way. And Buddy had been the devil. We were convinced that if we shaved his head we would see 666 embedded under his golden fur.

As we walked through the doors of Denny's, the first thing Michael asked the hostess before even saying hello was, "Do you serve beer?"

She studied us with a bizarre expression before she muttered a long drawn-out, "Yes."

Before she could even murmur another sentence Michael pretty much asked her to bring around six of them to our table—for starters. Evidently, she looked at him like he was kidding and voiced a small chuckle, but promptly noticed that Michael was not smiling or blinking for that matter.

Usually the waitress was the one that served your drinks, but I think the hostess sensed our desperation and brought the beers immediately without saying a word. That poor hostess probably had nightmares about the two psychopaths who walked in talking in monotone sentences and looking like hell.

Prior to this trip, we had never consumed alcohol at Denny's of all places. At this point, however, it was somewhat of a necessity as we had one more long, exhausting, headache-filled day to go. Thankfully, we did not get lost once due to Michael's great navigational skills. That was the one thing we had going for us. Had it been up to me, we would still be on the road today trying to find Las Vegas.

After our beer-drinking binge, things seemed to be a bit better. (Doesn't it always seem to work that way?) We were able to pass out and sleep through the night. Since the next day was supposed to be only a short, six-hour drive to Las Vegas, we did not leave at six in the morning as we had done the previous three days.

We were able to relax, sleep in a bit, and leave a little later. We were in a slightly better place mentally, though Buddy was still the same. Six hours in the car with him seemed like a lifetime. My only hope was that we would be able to survive one more horrific day.

Chapter 10-Vegas, baby!! March 6, 2006

It has been said that change is good. I don't remember anyone saying it was easy.

I never dreamt that I would be so happy to drive over the Hoover Dam. Our Las Vegas house was now only about an hour away. Finally, we'd made it. Four days had seemed like an eternity. We both felt as though we had aged ten years. It was hard to believe that just four days prior we were living in New York, and now we were starting all over again in Las Vegas, Nevada.

When we finally arrived, we let the dogs venture through their new home and showed them the potty area, which they learned right away. We were happy to have our dogs' cooperation for that reason. It did not take much to get them acclimated.

Once that was all taken care of, we started the strenuous but necessary task of unpacking our van. After a few exhausting hours of unloading everything, dragging boxes into the house, and lugging them up the stairs, we noticed something small and pink toward the front end of the inside of the van. It was scattered all over the front and clearly embedded into the tiny threads of the carpet.

As we investigated a little deeper, I remember shaking my head, closing my eyes, and taking a deep breath. I then looked toward the house where Buddy was staring at me through the window and shook my head again. I felt my body tense up and the muscles in my jaw start to clench. I think that was the point when I began the habit of talking to myself in a wide variety of meaningless obscenities.

On the floor in front of me, rooted deep into the carpet was four days' worth of what was supposed to be the one thing that was to save us, the one strategy that we so carefully planned out, the sure-fire sleep aid that would calm Buddy down: Benadryl!

He had not swallowed any of them. Not one. There were close to sixteen pills on the floor of that van, melted and rooted deep into the carpet. He took his pill pocket cookie, ate the cookie, and though I could swear I watched him eat the whole thing, he had spitefully spit out each and every single Benadryl tablet.

I immediately had a flashback to years ago when he was on his puppy Prozac and how they did not seem to affect him. I wondered if they had not worked because he'd spit those out as well. Would his previous owners find them crushed up in a corner upon cleaning the basement one day? Would the same feelings of anxiety and disbelief flow through their body like a never-ending stream? This freaking dog!

While that did explain a few things, it certainly did not make me any happier. There was nothing more embarrassing or frustrating like having a dog outsmart you...once again. I did not consider myself to be a genius, but I did like to take the liberty of saying I was definitely smarter than a dog; however, I was truly beginning to second-guess myself.

We had lost it. We were dangerously close to our breaking point. It was imperative that we left and ate lunch. We got away from the dogs, regrouped, started over, and tried to forget the nightmare of the past four days. After all, we were starting our new life in Vegas. Michael had his job from New York, though slightly modified, and I was, for the moment, unemployed.

I did not realize what a vulnerable position that was until we settled into our new home. We made sure Michael had his job and did not really concern ourselves with me. Looking back today, four years later, I am not sure I would be so daring—especially with the job market and the unstable economy. I am glad we had the courage to do it though; otherwise, we would have never gotten here.

After a few weeks of searching the job-boards, I was able to land a job part-time for a somewhat egotistical man whom I really did not respect or like. That did not last too long, and I actually got fired for taking days off. I had never been outright fired before, but it was rightfully so. I was only working two days per week, and I took those two days off. I just was not that into it, and it was quite far from our house. If I had not gotten fired, I most likely would have quit. It was just a matter of time.

After a few more searches, interviews, and mandatory drug tests (most jobs in Las Vegas require them), I landed a job at a popular employment staffing agency. It would have been decent; however, it was not in my line of work. The job was as a recruiter for computer-related fields, but my expertise was in technology, not recruiting, so this did not help me much.

I stuck it out until something better came along, but I could not wait to leave. The hours were long, and it was very different from what I was accustomed to. Michael had to constantly listen to me complain about traffic from this job (near The Strip) to our house fifteen miles away. I think he secretly could not wait for me to quit.

During this job search, we were also searching for another house. The one where we were residing was quaint, practical, and served its purpose, but it was just a bit small for two adults and two large dogs. The yard gave them no room whatsoever to stretch their legs.

There was also a disturbing incident that got me extremely livid—enough so that I did not need to think twice about moving.

Michael was out of town, and my neighbor was having a private family party. I was sitting on our couch in the living room, enjoying a peaceful night of watching a movie on television with my dogs lying on either side of me. Our front window facing the normally quiet street was open, and a gentle, warm breeze was flowing through.

A few hours into the neighbor's party, their two five-year-old girls were outside and kept running in front of my window, making the dogs bark and go crazy. The girls would then run away. Five seconds later, they would come back and repeat the same thing.

I tried to be patient; after all, they were just kids, but the more I sat there and allowed my peaceful night to get interrupted, the angrier I was getting at the parents. Where were they and why were these kids allowed to roam free after dark?

After about another three minutes of this repetitive nonsense, I lost my otherwise calm demeanor. My patience level had dwindled to zero, as I really did not appreciate anyone tormenting my dogs or myself, for that matter.

I quietly went outside, and just as I did, I overheard the kids say to each other, "Let's throw rocks at the dogs!" They were planning to throw rocks at my dogs. That was just simply not going to happen. At that point, I really did not care that they were five years old. I went over there, and in the nicest tone that I could muster, I let the kids know that they will not ever throw rocks at the dogs and to knock it off immediately. To my amazement, they listened and ran into the backyard. The parents were still nowhere to be found.

Not wanting to ruin the owner's party and since the issue seemed to have been resolved, I patiently waited until the next day to speak to him. I wanted to let him know about his kids and their grand plan. I politely explained to him that they were purposely annoying the dogs, and had I not gone outside, they were going to throw rocks through my window and at my innocent dogs. I shudder to think of what would have happened if I had not been home.

His response still makes me cringe and gets me angry until this very day.

He said, "I know. They terrorize our dog, too. That is the problem with Vegas, the rocks."

I think if I were a man I would have knocked him out right there on the spot. The rocks were the problem? How about parents who did not take responsibility or correct their children? Had I not been home, my window would have been shattered and my dogs possibly stoned to death? How was that acceptable?

I did not have a problem with children making mistakes or even bad judgment calls. I did get upset when the parents were not there to correct them and apologize for their actions or, better yet, blame inanimate objects such as rocks as the problem.

This was reason enough for me to move. That, coupled with the tiny living space, made the decision easy for us.

We found a really nice area in which to live, and as luck would have it, they were building brand new homes. After checking out the area a bit, we decided to sell our current home and put a down payment on this new one. It was still far enough from The Strip that we did not need to deal with the heavy traffic, but close enough to visit if we ever felt the need.

It was a pretty nice house, located on a nice-sized yard (by Vegas standards). There were a few parks, including a dog park, as well as stairs leading to an endless hiking trail.

After we moved into the house in November of 2006, I found an ideal job providing tech support for a software company. This seemed to be most fitting for me. It was about a half-hour from our new house and was close enough to what I was seeking in the job market. The manager and I hit it off from the start, as she was also a dog-lover and shared the same offbeat sense of humor.

I was able to start immediately, and this fit right into our plan. It was starting to come together as we had hoped. Our new house was great and our neighbors were starting to move in as well. Buddy's antics, however, did not stop there.

I received an interesting phone call while I was at work one day. Michael called me up and in a curious tone and asked me a very odd question.

"Do you own a black slipper?"

I thought about it for a minute, and with a weird feeling in the pit of my stomach, replied, "Um, no. Why?"

He said matter-of-factly that Buddy had ventured out of our house while the maintenance guys were over doing work inside of our house. The front door did not shut tight unless you slammed it, and Buddy sneaked out. When he came back, he was slobbering all over a random black slipper. I could not imagine where he had gotten it from and my mind was racing with possibilities.

While I was speaking to Michael trying to figure it out, Michael abruptly exclaimed that he had to hang up as someone was knocking at the door and he would call me back.

Knowing Buddy as well as I did, I could only guess where he had retrieved this new item. Sure enough, Michael called me back hysterically laughing. At this point, my imaginative juices were flowing. What the hell had this dog done now?

In between fits of laughter, Michael was able to fill me in with the entire story. Always the opportunist, Buddy had snuck out of our house and leisurely walked into our neighbor's garage while our new neighbor was moving in. Buddy then proceeded to look around and steal his slipper right out of one of the boxes. He barked that famous I-stole-something-come-chase-me bark, brought it back into our house, and sat on the couch as if he'd done nothing wrong.

Though I was not there to see his face, I am sure Buddy was gleaming with pride. The world was his playground and he probably felt that he was entitled to play with his new toy.

That knock at the door happened to be our neighbor standing there looking kind of perplexed with the other matching slipper in his hand. I can only envision what he must have been thinking as he was moving into his new house.

There he was, innocently unpacking his boxes of household items such as dishes, clothes, and, of course, slippers. Out of nowhere, a psychotic dog had run up and not attacked him, but instead had stolen from him right under his nose and run away.

And so it began. Buddy was terrorizing the new neighborhood. We were very lucky that our new neighbor turned out to be so friendly and such a dog lover, so there were no hard feelings. We were lucky because Buddy did something similar about two years later.

Again, though we should have learned the first time, we took the pups for a walk and when we came back, the same neighbor was in the front yard of his house. We all said hello, talked for a while, and started to go into our respective houses. We let Buddy off of the leash since we did not live on a busy street anymore and figured he was tired from his two-mile walk.

Almost everyone in Las Vegas uses their garage as an entryway to their house, and just as we were entering our garage, we saw Buddy glance toward our neighbor's house. With Buddy, one certain look, and you know you are in for it. You just never know exactly how much you are in for.

Our neighbor had just entered his house from the door leading from the garage to his house with his garage door open. We noticed the look in Bud's eyes, and faster than we could grab him, he ran over to our neighbor's house and patiently waited outside the door to his house. Before I could reach him our unsuspecting neighbor came back out to shut his garage door, and Buddy raced past him into the entrance of his house.

This normally would not be so bad, except for the fact that our neighbor had a dog that did not particularly like other dogs, especially those that barged in unannounced. Once again, Buddy, now eight years old, had trespassed into our neighbor's house.

If you have ever tried to remove a dog from a place they do not want to be removed from, you will know what I mean when I say this was not easy. Buddy had himself in a down position, rolled over with his belly exposed. All four legs were trying to push me off, and his tail was wagging like an electric fan. To add to this, he was playfully biting my wrists so that I couldn't grab him. Clearly he was having a ball. I wish I could have said the same for me.

After a good chase, no harm was done, and I was able to carry this now seventy-pound monster out of the house. Once again, I felt my face turn beet red from embarrassment, and my back was aching from carrying a crazy, determined, squirming dog.

After this episode, I did not want to face our neighbor for a few days because I felt like I always did when Buddy caused havoc: run-down, beaten, and embarrassed.

Through all of this, we learned how to deal with some of his craziness, and some of it we just never understood. Since we had first adopted Buddy, he had calmed down a great deal and listened to his commands more often than not. Some things would never change, however, as he still maintained his persistent desire to be somewhat ill-behaved.

Regardless of his interesting conduct, we were happy with our decision to move to Las Vegas, and especially thrilled that our neighbors were so friendly.

Things were going extremely well until a repeat of the issues with rocks came into play.

Chapter 11-More Rocks?

Tolerance is definitely an acquired trait. It is something that needs to be practiced and perfected. It definitely does not happen overnight.

About a year after living in our new home, I was making my lunch and the dogs were outside barking continuously with no end in sight. As I looked in the backyard, it was easy to see what was setting them off.

Behind us no houses had been built yet, and it was an empty lot—an improvised playground where kids could easily get injured. Hanging off of the brick fence in our backyard that day were two small kids.

I kindly asked the kids to get down as they were going to get hurt, and they blatantly ignored me. I asked them once more, and they proceeded to remain exactly where they were—only this time they threw a rock at one of the dogs.

That was it. That was all I needed to see. I had a flashback to the neighbor at our old house who'd said, "That's the problem with Vegas—the rocks," and I thought I was going to go ballistic on these kids. I let the dogs in the house, turned off the stove, and jumped into my car, driving full speed around the corner to find the parents.

Unleashing anger to the parents that really should have been directed at our previous neighbor, I started screaming, "Are those your kids? Look where they are. Do you know what they are doing? They threw rocks at my dogs. Control your kids!"

I'm sure I spit out some other nasty obscenities, sped away like a lunatic, and went back home, heart racing and mad as hell.

What was wrong with Las Vegas? How was it possible that this had happened twice in one year?

After brooding for a few hours, I finally calmed down. As the day progressed, I somewhat forgot about it, even though I was still fuming every time that I recalled the incident.

Toward the middle of the next day I heard a knock at the door. Not expecting anyone, I answered the door, and there in front of me was the mom, dad, the two kids, and their ten-year-old, adorable dog. With tears in her eyes, the mom apologized profusely and told me that her kids had something to say to me.

I knelt down to an apologetic little girl and boy, who promptly said, "We're sorry we threw rocks at your dogs." The little girl held her hand out. In it, she had rawhides that she'd brought for our dogs and said, "Please forgive us."

I nearly started bawling my eyes out. The mother and husband apologized and brought their dog to show me that they were not monsters and that they had a dog, too, so they understood. They did not intentionally mean to hurt the dogs.

I had so much anger toward our previous neighbors; I had taken it all out on this poor woman. I apologized up and down and explained that I was not psychotic but just assumed that she was also going to start blaming rocks for all of the world's problems.

We saw them on walks after that day and they were truly such friendly people. I felt so horrible. I learned not to jump to conclusions and act psychotic from that point on. I just could not tolerate anyone being mean to my dogs...especially when the dogs did not deserve it.

Living in a new place was definitely something I had to get used to. I was beginning to think everyone in that town had lost their minds, so I was glad that this second episode had ended a little more reasonably than the first.

If it hadn't, I think we would have had to endure another road trip—right back to New York!

Chapter 12- Miscellaneous Oddities

All of us are guilty of having some type of idiosyncrasy that separates us from others and makes us completely unique. Some...have more than the rest.

After living with Buddy for a number of years, we had accepted the fact that he was different and that every day he would surprise us with something new.

We knew he had some fears, but we just did not realize how drastically they affected him. While Buddy was not afraid of rain itself, thunderstorms brought a whole new meaning to the word "psycho."

It was quite common and natural for dogs to be afraid of thunder. To them, the harsh, loud banging sound was amplified, and there was no physical object for them to observe where the obtrusive sound was coming from. Typical of a lot of dogs, Buddy and thunder just did not mix. He became so frantic that he would seek shelter in confined places, such as the bathtub, somehow thinking this was safe.

One day he even busted into the closet, which had been closed. Somehow, he opened the door, jumped on top of all of the boxes we had on the floor, rummaged through them, and stomped on our brand new picture frames. Shattered shards of glass were strewn all over the place.

When we initially walked into the house from work, we knew something was up. Buddy was acting weird and moping with his tail tucked between his wobbly legs.

The thunderstorm had long subsided, so we did not even take into consideration the fact that he still might be frightened. As we slowly ascended up the stairs, my heart flip-flopped, as at first glance it appeared as if our house had been burglarized.

Pieces of glass and ripped boxes were all over the place. Miraculously, Buddy did not have so much as a scratch on him. I wish I could say the same for what was in those boxes.

After cleaning up most of the mess, I transferred everything to a sturdier crate and put them higher where Buddy could not get hurt in the event of another horrifying thunderstorm.

As if thunder were not bad enough, the rain was another story. Anytime it rained in New York, he refused to go outside to take care of business. It did not matter if he was holding it in for ten hours, he simply would not go. Worrying that this was inhumane and unhealthy, Michael decided to walk him in the front yard on a leash, taking shelter under a huge pine tree.

From that day forward, that is where Buddy peed in the event that it rained. Though Las Vegas did not accumulate much rain, this peculiar habit continued to hold true. On the rare occasion that it rained, Buddy got to pee in the front yard. We gave up understanding why this makes him happy, but like everything else with him, if it worked, we did not question it. I was quite sure our neighbors might question it a little and find it quite odd but there was just too much to explain when it came to this dog.

Some people told us in the gentlest of ways that they could never deal with a dog with as many quirks as Buddy. Especially when we spoke with someone who was not a dog lover, they just did not get it. To them, it was "just a dog."

When you are a dog lover, you get it. You understand that there is nothing in the world like communicating with a totally different species. No matter what you look like, sound like, or act like, your dog is going to love you unconditionally. You could buy them a mansion or live in a cardboard shack, and your dog will not care either way, as long as they are with you.

This is not because they are stupid as I have heard some ignorant people claim. If you think about it, we speak a completely different language than dogs, yet they can understand a wide variety of words. I cannot even put a number to the amount of words our dogs have understood. Yet, by the same token, we have no real clue what they are saying. And we are supposed to be the smart ones?

In addition, the nonverbal communication is truly amazing—and this goes for both human and canine.

As an example, Buddy and Brandi knew when we were planning to go for a walk, even if we were still sitting down, but just talking about going. It was not because we said the word "walk" as we so cleverly learned to spell everything out.

It was not due to routine, as we would sometimes break midday or some random time out of the norm and take them. They just knew our body language and would get up and walk to the closet where their leashes were kept. This was before we even put our sneakers on.

They also knew when we were finished eating at the table by listening to our forks hit the plate. The list could go on and on.

Even though Buddy was crazy, he was smart enough to know when it was absolutely necessary to behave. This happened a few times, but one that stood out was when I was home recovering from a major surgery.

A few years back I awoke in the middle of the night with what felt like an elephant sitting on my chest, and I could not catch my breath. It felt like I had to keep yawning, yet I did not have any pain. I just could not breathe well. Of course, I started panicking and that just made it more difficult, but I did not pass out. At the same time, I could not fall back asleep.

I was apparently functioning okay, even though I was exhausted, but still I could not get the breathing thing down. I did not fear a heart attack as I did not possess any of the symptoms that I had read about (other than the elephant on my chest), and my blood pressure was its normal low. I did, however, fear a life-threatening disease and thought for sure that the end was near.

After about a week of suffering through this, I grudgingly decided to stop being stubborn. With much hesitation, I gave in and went to the doctor. The technician took a few x-rays, listened to my breathing, and narrowed it down to pneumonia. Once they had prescribed some antibiotics, they sent me on my way.

I felt that this was a bit weird, as I was not coughing at all and aside from wanting to breathe, I did not feel sick. I really did not feel like pneumonia was the correct diagnosis, but who was I to question it? I did not have a degree in medicine like they did, so they must have known what they were talking about, right?

Two weeks passed, and I still could not breathe right. The prescribed medicine did absolutely nothing. I almost felt as if it made things worse than what they were from when the symptoms had first occurred.

Once I went back to the doctor, they solemnly suggested that I see a pulmonologist, as they did not know what was showing on my lungs. They took dozens of blood tests, x-rays, CAT scans, MRI's, a tuberculosis test, and many breathing tests in which I always tested okay.

Somehow, my oxygen level was perfect, yet I was still having these mysterious issues. The more frequently I had to visit the doctor, the crazier with panic I had become. The doctor actually had textbooks open on his desk trying to analyze what was wrong with me. The CAT scans did show something, but no one knew exactly what it was.

After six months of visiting doctors, laboratories, and technicians, my doctor mentioned that he thought I had B.O.O.P. This was the acronym for some obscure lung disease that I had never heard of before: bronchiolitis obliterans organizing pneumonia. He explained to me what it was, but he needed to put me under for surgery to get a definitive answer.

I had since cleverly nicknamed him Dr. Death. For some reason, I don't think he was too appreciative of that.

I had successfully avoided surgery my entire life, so needless to say, I was extremely unhappy with his preliminary prognosis and recommendation. I went to visit another doctor for a second opinion, but they agreed that exploratory surgery was necessary.

I even tried to lie to myself and say that I felt better, but when I had to stop to catch my breath just from walking down the hallway, I realized that I had no other choice.

The first surgery required that a tube with a camera attached be inserted down my throat. This was to try and see if there were any definitive clues explaining what was wrong with me.

They found nothing.

The doctors claimed that this was "somewhat good news" because if it were something bad, it would have easily shown up. I was happy about that, but I still had to endure the second surgery which was considered to be "major exploratory surgery" to achieve a proper diagnosis. There was a biopsy taken from my lung, and

I was kept in the hospital for three days spending some time in the Intensive Care Unit. I was terrified of what they might find.

It turned out that it was not B.O.O.P, but a lesser-known and just as undesirable disease, Sarcoidosis: a rare autoimmune lung disease that causes a type of inflammation in one or both lungs. There are different strains, some worse than others. No one knows what causes it, and no one knows how to cure it. Sometimes it stays for life, and sometimes it disappears by itself. Some people diagnosed with it live a normal life, and some people can die. When I acquired this information, I felt like I was in the middle of some sadistic type of nursery rhyme where the prime focus was to torture the person unlucky enough to read it.

When I arrived home from the hospital, I was prescribed a potpourri of medications. I was to take a few doses of Vicodin to help ease the pain of the surgery, along with some Prednisone to reduce the inflammation. Prednisone was like putting out a fire with gasoline; it cured one thing but had the ability to create other ailments that are much worse. Once home, I was supposed to rest for a week without doing anything strenuous.

To my astonishment, during that week Buddy did not jump on me or scratch or demand to play fight. He did not bark, cry, or complain at all. He gently crawled on top of the couch where I was sleeping, not once coming close to my stitches, and still managed to lie on top of me. Buddy was always a cuddle dog from day one. He could not just lie next to you; he had to be as much as on top of you as he could. During this time, he did not wake me up at all for the entire week and was gentle as a lamb. As soon as I recovered, however, he returned back to his old relentless self.

There are certain body communications that can be read by dogs, and Buddy sensed he had to be on his best behavior during that time. I found it both sweet and amazing. How did he know?

Similarly, reading his body language was just as easy. One morning we were walking on a trail down the block from our new house. The trail went for miles and miles and we were just coming back from a lengthy walk. Normally, Buddy and Brandi get to roam free on this path, but this time I had them on the leash as two joggers were passing us and sometimes people got irritated if the dogs were not properly restrained. I took notice of the men jogging as they had their heads held high and looked kind of snooty.

Well, Buddy looked at the joggers, and as they passed, Buddy looked at me and then at his leash. I laughed as I knew exactly what he wanted, so I rolled up the leash and handed it to him. He happily took his leash in his mouth, and then in the funniest gait I had ever seen Buddy carry out, he jogged with his head held high following the same body posture of the joggers. It may sound crazy, but if you knew him you would understand. Buddy was imitating the exact posture of the joggers. He then turned back to me and gave me his leash. He just wanted to be a clown for a few minutes, the only way Buddy knew how.

Dogs possess such a profound innocence. I mean this for all dogs. They are never purposely malicious. You can argue that dogs have been known to attack or even kill, and that is certainly true, but if you look at the circumstances surrounding those instances, there are usually legitimate reasons for it. Typically, it is because they are obeying their master and their master's sick way of training or they are physically sick. It could also be due to them being in the wild on their own for too long and it is instinct to protect what is theirs. They just have not been taught otherwise. Either way, it is never out of cold blood that a dog will attack, which is more than I can say for some people.

Buddy had always been on the mischievous side, but was a genuine sweetheart with the best of intentions. There was something about him which I have never figured out that made other dogs at ease with him. It just made me love him even more. I have read that if a dog is docile, trainers will put more excitable dogs to be trained amongst the calm dog so the nervous ones feel at ease. Well, Buddy was not a mellow dog by any means, yet other dogs loved to be around him.

An interesting situation presented itself back in New York. We were taking Buddy for a walk and we noticed this pit bull (which at the time, I thought were vicious) squirm under a broken picket fence. He then ran at top speed toward Buddy. My heart was racing, and I was frantic for words. I tried to advise Michael what to do, as I was the one holding Buddy, but I just could not think fast enough. Part of me wanted Michael to try to get the owner; the other part of me wanted Michael to stay to fight off this crazed pit bull. I was frozen with panic and thought for sure due to all of the pit bull hype that I had heard, that Buddy was as good as dead.

I looked at Buddy and then at this dog racing toward us and noticed one simple thing. Buddy was as calm as ever. His tail wagged, but he wasn't jumping or barking. He was just standing there nonchalantly smelling the grass. The two dogs' meeting was so uneventful, I was in disbelief. The vicious pit bull came over and smelled Buddy. Buddy smelled the pit bull and demonstrated the proper dog greeting. He then went back to smelling the grass like they were old friends enjoying a summer walk. Soon after, the pit bull ran home and tumbled back under his broken fence. That was my first real encounter with a pit, and I have loved them ever since. Sure they can be vicious, but as with all dogs, bad training is the main reason for that. Generally I have known them to be big mushes. With any dog, you have to be careful as you do not know their temperament or how they were brought up—but isn't that the same with people?

A few short months later, we had another frightening episode, this time featuring an Akita. Again we had taken Buddy for a walk and saw this giant dog coming at us.

A girl screamed at us, "Don't let him near your dog! Do not let him near your dog. He will attack! Get your dog away!"

Well, Einstein, not much we could do at that point. The dog was chasing us, not the other way around.

Ironically the girl was taking her sweet time. If I were not so scared for Buddy, I would have screamed at the girl for not getting to us in a more expedient manner. I grabbed Buddy so he was on two legs (probably the worst thing I could have done) in an effort to protect him from the wild beast upon us.

Wouldn't you know it, though, this Akita did the same thing as the pit bull and just smelled Buddy and walked away.

It has been said that dogs learn a ton of information from what we humans consider a disgusting habit of smelling each other's butt. They can determine if the dog is sick, scared, happy, etc. This is one reason why dogs tuck their tail between their legs when they are frightened. They do not want other dogs to know they are fearful, and this is sort of a defense mechanism for them. Though not the way that I would want to say hello, it is considered "rude" in dog world if they do not partake in this greeting, sort of similar to a handshake amongst humans. All I can gather is that when they smelled Buddy, they sensed that he was a friendly dog and not a threat to them. I can only hope that we are always that lucky when approached by other dogs.

Chapter 13-Another One?

There are too many dogs roaming free out there, partly due to negligence on the part of the owners. Unfortunately, there are only so many dogs that can be saved. Dogs cannot speak, so, when possible, it is up to us to speak up for them.

Year two of living in Las Vegas, I discovered that there was a no-kill shelter in town and planned to go check it out. I felt that if I could help with dogs in any way, it would be a perfect opportunity for me. In addition, I would get to socialize and meet some people that shared the same love of animals. My coworker volunteered as well. Many of the dogs there were surrendered by their owners or abandoned on the streets to take care of themselves.

A few weeks into it, my coworker brought one of the dogs she was fostering into work with her. It was listed as a golden-mix. Her name was Toffee and she was adorable. She was slightly smaller than a purebred golden, close to forty pounds, with a pink nose and what is known as monochromic eyes. Her eyes were the same exact light brown color of her coat. She was found on the streets of Las Vegas, apparently deserted by her previous owner.

Every week at the local pet store, they held adoptions, and that weekend my coworker said she would drop off Toffee and come back to collect her later. I offered to take her for the week and give fostering a try.

It was our luck that the first week was great, and we were having a lot of fun with our new little foster dog, until one night, out of the blue, Toffee became ill and came close to dying on us.

She could barely walk, and her body was actually vibrating, strangely enough. Though not always indicative of a fever, her nose was burning hot. It was three in the morning, and I could not console her or make her any better. I did not know what to do. It was not like she had been out of our sight at all, so she could not have gotten into anything that we did not know about or eaten anything that would have made her this sick.

I was somewhat notorious for being a worrywart if the dogs were sick, so I decided to wake Michael for his thoughts on the matter. I thought that maybe I was not thinking straight and her body really was not vibrating. When I saw a little panic in his eyes, I knew something was wrong. He said he would stay up with her for the next few hours, and we would rush her to the hospital at six when they opened. Unfortunately, nothing remotely nearby by was open at three in the morning.

That morning, Michael drove to the emergency animal hospital with a very lethargic Toffee lying on top of my lap. She barely moved, which was not like her, and her breathing was labored. She would occasionally acknowledge me holding her, but looked like she was fading fast.

Sure enough we arrived at the vet's office and Toffee's temperature was 105—three degrees higher than it should have been. We knew she was physically in trouble. After some more close examination, they had to perform emergency surgery, as she was suffering from a major infection stemming from when she was spayed.

The doctors said the surgery would be over within five hours and we would be able to take her home that day. We decided to go home and catch up on some sleep for a few hours. When we finally went back, she wound up being okay, but this resulted in her having three open holes in her stomach with a shoelace-type string weaved through them to keep them open. They were there to drain the infection site and had to remain open so that it kept draining.

If it sounds disgusting, that is because it certainly was. My new job was to flush these holes with medicine every three hours. I typically had a low tolerance for anything that involved flushing out holes in someone's stomach, but I found it in me to make concessions for this dog. It was not an easy thing to do as no dog really wants to lie still while you poured liquid in her belly. I was smart enough to trick her by giving her a rawhide while flushing the medicated liquid.

That week came and went, and Toffee came to live with us on a permanent basis. She also had different surgeries almost every year.

I just could not give her up. No one looked sane enough to adopt her, and I felt no one was better suited to keep her. I felt that if someone else had owned her, they would not have taken her to the hospital that night and she would have certainly died.

At adoptions, people walked over to the adoption fence and, to me, they just looked weird. By admission, I could probably be talking myself right into an insane asylum, but I did not like the way they were dressed, nor did I like their hairstyle, sunglasses, hat, or the way their toenails weren't clipped or had not been groomed.

Silly, I know, but true nonetheless.

No one looked as if they should own Toffee. A woman asked me if I could wake Toffee up so she could see her walk. I remember getting so angry and annoyed that this woman had the audacity to ask me to wake Toffee from her slumber. Needless to say, we adopted her in July of 2007—Toffee, not the woman!

Two years passed and she did have some issues, such as moles on her face and on her eyes that had to be removed. Tumors in her belly have also been removed, she has had a double mastectomy, and her teeth have been cleaned, as well.

While we were getting all of this work done at the vet, someone approached us and exclaimed, "Oh my God, you have a duck toller!"

Michael and I just looked at each other, and then turned toward this woman.

At the same time we both said, "A what?"

She promptly repeated herself. "A Nova Scotia duck tolling retriever."

Still clueless, we looked around and said, "No, sorry, this is a golden-mix." We thought the mix was with a pit bull because of the pink nose.

The woman turned out to be a groomer at the vet and went online right away to show us the breed. We had never heard of it before so had no idea what she was talking about. Sure enough, Toffee was no doubt a purebred duck toller. She had the exact markings as the dog on the Internet.

Chapter 14-And then there were three...

Lots of deep breaths and patience—that's how!

Some called us crazy for taking care of three dogs. Although Buddy was now in his senior years, still excitable, but manageable. Toffee was a bit of a handful, as well, as she displayed some possessive behavior from being out on the streets on her own for some time, coupled with incessant whining and a weird habit of continually licking the floor.

She went to training as much as time allowed and got somewhat better in her ways.

She was definitely a sweetheart of a dog, but was dumped in the desert by her previous owners and had to search for her own food. The end result was that she could be a bit possessive when it came to eating. I suppose that was what happened when dogs are needlessly abandoned.

Some of my training techniques were not conventional, but occasionally it did work. Buddy was almost considered well-behaved, and he was a completely different dog from when we first adopted him.

For Toffee, one of her main issues was that you couldn't pet her on the back, as she must have injured it during her days on the street. The x-rays showed a fusion of some vertebrae, and if you touched a certain spot too hard she would scream in pain. It did not necessarily hurt her if you pet her gently, but she would freak out when someone would try to pet her there.

With that, I decided to associate her back getting touched with something good. That something good consisted of a treat (Toffee was extremely food driven) along with me singing her a song that I made up—now available on the Internet for .ninety-nine cents. This was the one instance in my life where I had an audience that appreciated my horrible, off-key singing, but she loved it. (I was just kidding about my song being available. I would not torture anyone like that). She finally allowed us to pet her back with no issues. Her ears still perked up, but she didn't lash out and try to nip at us to stop.

She would, however, run to the cookie jar afterwards or look at you weird if you didn't sing.

The lessons I learned were that if you ever had a dog with some behavioral issues, and you read all of the books and took the training classes and were still having a problem, you shouldn't hesitate to think outside the box. That sometimes conventional thinking did not always work.

In certain situations, you had to think of the specific reasons for that particular dog's issues and work with them on an entirely new level. Every dog was different.

Another trick was to use the same training techniques as you would for a two-year-old child. For instance, Buddy's worst punishment was being alone. So, if he was being bad, we locked him in his room (his crate) for a few minutes and left the room.

All it took was a few minutes. Dogs lived in the moment, so there was never any need to extend this to any longer than ten minutes. He would then come out of his crate a little bit better behaved. He most likely would act up again later but we would just follow the same routine.

Funny enough, after a while of him acting up, he saw us get up to punish him and would run to his crate on his own.

As bad as Buddy was, Brandi was the exact opposite. Throughout the years with Brandi, I do not recall one instance where she needed to be punished. She would, however, go into her crate on her own when Buddy was sent to his and come out only when he was allowed to come out. She was also known to let Buddy out of his crate somehow while it was still locked. I do not know how she did it, but similar to how she used to let herself out, we just surmised that she adored him and took care of him—and that she was Houdini.

Dogs are amazing in the way they depend on and learn from each other. Brandi learned a lot from

Buddy, and Toffee learned a lot from both Buddy and Brandi.

From Brandi she learned not to mess with Brandi's toys or there would be hell to pay. Brandi would not bite, but she pushed Toffee to the ground when Toffee tried to take her toys, and Brandi just stood over her until Toffee learned not to mess with her. Then she cried every time Brandi went near her, although she did love to sleep with her.

Brandi, on the other hand, preferred to sleep by herself in the corner of the bed, next to no one. This in itself made Toffee cry because Toffee wanted to cuddle with her. Go figure.

From Buddy she learned how to play with toys and become another cuddle dog. When we first got Toffee, she was not used to being kissed, hugged, or played with. After being with us she grew to love her toys and to play, though you still had to be careful of her bumps on her belly and injuries on her back—another disadvantage of being dumped and abandoned in the desert by her previous family.

Lastly, from Toffee, Buddy learned to open doors that we closed half-way. Thanks, Toffee!

Chapter 15-The Three Musketeers

There is nothing like having true friends to rely upon every single day.

Though we have loved all three, Brandi was too perfect to write about as she never did anything wrong. She was the epitome of the most perfect dog. It was amazing how adopting a dog at six months made all of the difference in how well she behaved. Although, I think with Buddy, he just had it in him to be wild. Even if we did adopt him at an early age, I believe he would still be somewhat crazy. Toffee did plenty wrong, but she was not as crazy as Buddy. I have not met many dogs who even come close to sharing his energy level. He was in a class all by himself. I have owned dogs my whole life, and yet never had to work so hard to get one to listen and obey—especially when they knew exactly what it was that I was saying to them.

There were, however, a lot of endearing things about Buddy. These are things that most people who knew him never saw or would believe. For instance, when it came time to nap with Buddy, there was nothing like it. People only saw him when he was jumping, barking or misbehaving.

While he was sleeping, he literally liked to be spooned (I know, sounds kind of weird), but he loved to be hugged and cuddled while he slept. He loved to nestle his head right under my chin. All of his mischievous activities during the day were forgotten during the night. It made it all worthwhile.

In addition, it was interesting to watch him as he was always strategically thinking. For instance, we went on a walk one day down the trail from our house; this time he was on a leash. The trail was partly paved, and then off on either side there were plenty of rocks (of course, that is apparent in Vegas), cactus, and other types of wild brush. Sections of this trail veered off into the canyon and preserve, where coyotes ran in the distance, and some jackrabbits occasionally zipped by in front of us. This left us walking up hills on dirt paths. It was a great hiking trail and could be as strenuous or as moderate as you would like.

It was on this trail that Michael walked over off to the side to smell a beautiful purple wildflower on a cactus. Buddy wanted to follow, but I did not let him. I had no reason for not letting him; I just did not feel like wandering over there. We thought nothing of it and continued walking for about two miles and then turned back, this time with the dogs off of the leashes. As we passed that same cactus, Buddy roamed off of the path and smelled the exact same flower that Michael smelled an hour prior. He had to do it just because I would not let him earlier.

As you may have surmised, he had a very keen talent for getting his way. If Buddy wanted to play but we were just too busy to play with him, he knew what to do. In the dogs' toy chest were about one hundred toys, ranging from ripped-up shirts (one of Buddy's favorites from when he was a pup) to stuffed animals that squeak or talk to Kong toys, nyla-bones, baseballs, plastic toys, and more. Amongst them was a tennis ball, which we appropriately renamed the "attention ball."

Each of our dogs had their favorite toy. For Buddy, it was typically not a tennis ball. He just used this as a ploy to get the party started. He typically liked sneakers, cardboard boxes, toilet paper and paper towel rolls, and socks. Brandi usually loved tennis balls. Toffee had a plastic toy that no one had ever played with but had been with us from day one of Buddy's arrival. That was called her "baby toy," for lack of a better term.

We called the tennis ball the "attention ball" because Buddy held it and then barked his bark and sort of played ball with himself before surrendering it to Brandi. He looked irresistible and knew it, so he got attention any time he grabbed this ball.

It usually stopped us dead in our tracks as Brandi would then start playing hackey sack with it...literally. She would balance the ball on her two front paws while lying down and then throw it in the air and catch it. This usually sent Toffee off into puppy land where she would grab her toy and start growling with it and throwing it up into the air for attention. It was a regular circus.

Yet again, Buddy achieved what he originally set out to do, which was to get everyone in a good mood and have them play with him. He loved when the house was in an uproar and everyone was involved.

There were other things I cannot explain about Buddy so I claim they were a coincidence; although, a deeper, more spiritual part of me does not know if I truly believe that.

For example, Michael and I purchased a netbook from a local computer store. We'd had it for about three months but Michael still had the box on a table in his office. We were lying in bed one night, and Buddy was lying on the floor. The home shopping network was on the television, and we were watching an advertisement of the same netbook. As we were watching, Michael and I started a discussion, and he had asked me if it was the same specs as the one we had.

I replied, "I think so—it's probably listed on the box or on the paperwork." We started talking about the netbook and some of its features when no more than five minutes later, Buddy ran out of the room.

We thought nothing of it and just thought he was going to go downstairs to get some water. Within minutes, he ran back in, barking like a maniac with his famous trademark bark. There, in his mouth was the computer box we were just speaking of.

It is those weird occurrences that made him so unique and what compelled me to write about him.

The list goes on and on. He loved getting his teeth brushed. He loved Guinness beer, sans the beer cap (although beer is not good for dogs). He waited on the stairs for us to go to sleep and loved to help carry whatever it was we were carrying. He touched the hearts of almost everyone who met him, even after tormenting that very person.

He just had a knack for making people love him. My mother, for example, is not what you would call a dog lover. She likes them and would never hurt them, but is not crazy about them like we are.

As kids, we had enforced that we had at least two dogs at a time; however, my mom was probably never happy about that.

Buddy, whom my mother nicknamed "The Budster," had secretly become one of my mother's favorites. I witnessed for the first time in her life that she actually kissed Buddy on top of his head, although if you asked her, she would adamantly deny it. She always claimed kissing an animal was "gross."

In addition, Michael's father was not a dog fanatic by any means. He also had developed a bit of a soft spot for Buddy. While some may have been disgusted by touching Buddy's slobbered-on rawhide or chewed-up toy, Michael's dad didn't seem to mind and always initiated a little tug of war with Buddy whenever he came to our house. I recall him laughing at Buddy's original way of barking and how Bud would get so excited.

In addition, not many people were afraid of him, including strangers. Sometimes this worked in my favor, but other times, not so much. Michael was away one week and I was home alone when a solicitor knocked on our door. I had just battled traffic (okay, not that much traffic), and literally just walked in the door (well, like an hour prior). I was not in the mood to be sold anything. I did not even want to speak to anyone. I thought I was in the clear of being harassed with three dogs barking at the top of their lungs when I opened the door just a crack.

I used this to my advantage and told the gentleman that I was not interested, could not really hear him, and that I could not control my three very vicious dogs. Just as I was reciting my speech, Brandi appeared at the door wagging her tail with a pink bunny in her mouth, Toffee was holding her green, squeaky baby toy, and Buddy appeared at the door with a little pink heart-shaped pillow in his mouth. The guy just laughed at me as my face turned red, and he obnoxiously proclaimed that he could see how vicious they were. He then continued to ask if he could tell me about the product he was selling.

I walked outside somewhat annoyed that the dogs did not at least growl and pretend to be vicious, but held my ground. I was too involved now to back down. It was not even about the product, but I proceeded to lie even further, claiming, "They are vicious. They were just taught to bark with toys in their mouth." At least that was somewhat of a truth. They were taught to bark with toys in their mouth and Toffee could be vicious if you stole her bone. Other than that, I flat out lied. Guilty! I just wanted to be alone.

Aside from his non-watchdog behavior, Buddy definitely had a list of oddities (or perhaps it is me that is odd). When it was time for them to all go to the bathroom before bed, the girls went like clockwork; however, Buddy kind of just looked at us. I was in one my famous wacky moods and I do not know how I came up with it or why I even said it but one day, I said, "Buddy, the pee-pee monster is outside waiting for you." With that, he got up and went. It worked each and every time and I have no idea why. I guess there is proof that he did not understand what some words meant because monsters are generally supposed to be scary. Maybe in the dog world, that theory just does not hold true.

I did not always know what tactics would work training Buddy, but as the years went on, I learned. Some things were there the whole time we had Buddy, but we just did not catch.

For example, whenever we came back from shopping, Buddy always looked for something to carry in. We assumed he was looking for some type of toy, which we did not have, so we just ignored him, leaving him to mope away on his own.

One day, we gave him something to hold from one of the shopping bags so he would stop being a pest, and he loved it. That was all he wanted: something to carry. It did not have to be a toy. After that Buddy came outside with us to help with the packages all of the time. He patiently waited until we gave him something to carry into the house. It could be a small box, or an English muffin package, or anything he could fit in his mouth. He would bring it inside and hand it back to us, and then keep coming out with us until all of the packages are inside of the house.

It was this type of thing that can't quite be explained to people without getting a blank stare that translates into "Are you serious?" It is also this type of thing that we grew to love.

Chapter 16-Senior Years

I've noticed him slowly turn gray around the eyes and nose and while some may say he looks like he has gotten old, I notice that he has only become more beautiful. Prior to Buddy, I have never in my life met anyone, human or canine, who has so much love in his heart...or who gives it away so freely.

I have wanted to write this for a long time and one of my main goals of writing it was to make sure Buddy was alive when I finished it. Upon writing my last word, I wanted to make sure Buddy was sitting on the couch next to me like he does every night.

If you personally do not know me and you are reading this, that means I chose to publish this book and succeeded. If not, it will serve as a memoir to me of one of the most precious and special times of my life.

I often wonder how our lives would have been drastically different if we had chosen not to adopt Buddy on that cold day in December. Though he is "only a dog" as I have heard so many unknowing people say, he has taught both Michael and me countless life lessons and has been with us through every major decision we ever had to make. We have gone through many adventures that without Buddy I'm not so sure we would have taken the time to explore.

What would have happened to Buddy? Would he have found another family that could deal with him and his constant clowning around? Would he have gone into a cold and lonely shelter where he would meet an untimely death at not even two years old? Would we even think about him all these years later as that crazy dog we "almost" adopted, similar to the wild, discounted puppy in the pet store?

Sometimes the path that you choose is not always an easy one, but the rewards that you gain from it are worth all of the hard work. Adopting Buddy and dealing with his crazy antics and oddities every day have by far outweighed the many headaches he has given us.

As he and Brandi get older, and their muzzles are now covered in a gray mask instead of the golden puppy face, I have noticed that there is certain knowledge that I think only an older dog possesses.

Now that they have grown out of their puppy years and are maturing into their senior years, it has all started to make sense to them, as well.

Buddy tried his hardest to turn Michael and me certifiably insane. When he realized that did not happen (though there is still time), Buddy finally learned that we loved him unconditionally. Nothing he did was going to make us give him away like his previous three owners had.

There are times when we only have to give him a look or even a nod, and he knows what we are expecting from him. Similarly, there are times when he does the same, and we know what he wants. Over the years, we have developed such a strong bond with our dogs and do not regret our decision to adopt one bit.

Though I am sorry for how Buddy's beginning years started out, I am entirely grateful for the gift that his previous owners bestowed upon us. I can only hope they have found as much love, happiness, understanding, knowledge, and laughter as we have with Buddy.

Sometimes life does not have to be so serious, and Buddy has always made sure that we knew that wholeheartedly. I hope when the time does come for him to leave us on this earth without him, that we will be able to remember that lesson and carry it on for him.

He is ten years old now and we are hoping he is with us for a few more years. He is still crazy, though somewhat slower. He still goes for at least a mile-walk every day, still steals every day, and makes us laugh and yell at him every single day. It is a bit heartbreaking when we see him only jogging down the path, versus when he was able to outrun anyone on that schoolyard back in New York.

Though there are not many rabbits where we now live, occasionally we see one hopping along, and while Buddy used to love chasing them in the past, he now sort of takes a few quick steps and then happily goes back to his walk. It takes him a bit longer to walk up the stairs, though he can still make it. If he is trying to jump on the couch, he just stops and pauses a little, but all in all, he is still such a happy and funny dog. His beautiful smile brightens any day.

Sometimes, he still acts so much like a puppy that we forget he is ten. He loves to demonstrate this to us, especially at the playground down the block from our house. While no one is looking (since dogs are not allowed), we take our dogs there as Brandi loves to go on the slide. While they are there, it is like they are still youngsters. You would never realize their true ages. Brandi tries to go down the slide, and he chases her around. He gets a little protective whenever Brandi does anything daring. Believe it or not, both he and Toffee do not possess that daredevil mentality. Brandi, on the other hand, does. She finds it fun to slide down the twisted slides while Buddy barks and carries on until she has safely landed on the spongy ground.

After they come home, they usually jump on the couch and take a nap. As I look upon Buddy sleeping, I am thankful each and every day about our decision to keep him. Time goes so fast, and it feels like a lifetime ago that we adopted him, and for him it was a lifetime. He was always such a maniac, but the message he conveys is simple: stop and smell the roses—or in his case, the pretty cactus flowers. Life is too short.

Though generally misunderstood, he is and always will be a special little boy. I wish I could fully adapt to his way of thinking and apply it to my own life. To Buddy, in his little world, there is no evil. Everyone is good and has the best of intentions.

Enjoy life, play a lot, and be free. Make people laugh and always initiate a good time. When you see someone is down and depressed, do something to take their mind off of it and leave their worries elsewhere. Do not take no for an answer and be sure to drive people a little crazy if you get the chance. If I could speak for Buddy (and I sometimes believe that I could), I guarantee that would be part of his life's motto.

While he is alive now, we know one day he won't be here to cause havoc. We think about the void that will take place in our life the day that Buddy is gone. We think about how we are going to help Brandi live happily without her partner in crime. Toffee has only known him for two years, but has grown to love him and seeks him out to lie next to if Brandi does not want to be bothered. If you are reading this now or ten years from now, Buddy's spirit will always live on. He will make it known that he still needs and demands to be loved no matter which world he is living upon.

I think one of the hardest reminders we will have to endure when he is gone is seeing our shoes in the exact place that we left them. In the past years that we have owned him, I never had a morning where my shoes were easily found.

My mornings usually consist of me screaming to Michael "Babe—is my left, black shoe upstairs?"

To which he'd yell down, "Yeah. Is my blue sneaker down there?" This was something we are able to count on each and every morning, and it is going to be sorely missed when he is gone. I have a feeling he is not going to go quietly and will find a way to hide our sneakers from Heaven and pleasantly haunt us from wherever he ends up. I truly hope that he does.

If you have a dog, take a moment to appreciate and love them. You'll be happy you did. Unfortunately, their time on this earth goes by way too quickly, but the valuable lessons they teach us can last a lifetime.

Small Tangent...and I Promise I'll Stop

Opening your home and your heart to an animal in need is truly a great experience. Just make sure it is the right experience for you.

I have to write this, and then I will stop. One thing that kills me is people who adopt or purchase a puppy as either a toy for their child or just because it is cute only to dispose of it when their child gets bored or the cute puppy turns into a dog and they realize it is actually a lot of work taking care of a dog.

Though they cannot speak in what humans call language, dogs do communicate in their own way, they do have feelings, and they do not understand why their family would just get rid of them.

It is not like you can explain the reasons to a dog. You just can't. To them, they have just been abandoned and although they can adapt and find a new family (if they are lucky enough to get adopted), they still suffer from major separation anxiety. It is a real issue, not something that someone just made up. Dogs do get upset when they no longer have their master. They also get upset when they were domesticated and now have to learn to fight the elements and hunt for their own food.

There are so many dogs in shelters today. Some are lucky enough to find a new family. Some spend their days and nights in boarding facilities in hopes of finding a family, while others have the unfortunate experience of getting euthanized way before their due time.

I have heard so many horror stories of the things these dogs have had to endure. I feel it is our job as responsible humans to speak on behalf of these poor animals.

Though I love dogs, I often try to dissuade people from getting one unless they are prepared to handle the following:

1. Puppies get big. Make sure you have the adequate space to handle your dog's expected size.
2. Dogs bark. I have actually heard of people returning or abandoning dogs because they bark. Really? Is this not common knowledge?
3. Dogs drool.
4. Dogs sometimes do not have manners.
5. They may have an accident on your rug. They may also have one if they get excited.
6. They may jump on the furniture.
7. They shed.

8. They do have waste that needs to be disposed of—by you.
9. They may have behavioral issues that you have to deal with.
10. Vet bills may get very high.
11. Some dogs need very expensive food (ahem, Toffee) as their stomachs can't handle regular food.
12. They may live to be eighteen!!
13. Dogs chew things. Sometimes it is things that they should not chew.
14. Dogs steal.
15. Dogs need to be groomed.
16. They may get sick at inopportune moments.
17. They may counter surf. This means they may steal things of importance off of your counter.
18. Taking care of a dog is a lot of work.
19. Some do need to be exercised constantly, depending on the breed.
20. There are many other surprises that are too numerous to list.

When adopting, there are so many different instances that can happen. We knew Buddy was a problem child, but we never imagined the many situations he would put us in. Still, we would not change it for the world. I cannot imagine what our life would have been like if we had not adopted Buddy. We are guilty of not doing all of the research prior to adopting, but we sort of made up for it along the way by trying to rectify unpredictable issues. The commitment was there, only the knowledge was not. In the end it paid off. As with everything, hopefully the lessons that we learned will not go forgotten.

If you are not one hundred percent sure that you could handle a dog, then just wait until you are ready. There will never be a shortage of dogs, so if the time is not right, then do not adopt. That is the best advice I can give.

I would love for everyone to help save lives, but it may not be the right fit for everyone. I could sit here and list one thousand positive reasons for owning a pet, but you have to be ready to embrace it; otherwise, it simply is not good for you or the dog.

I have to reiterate here for anyone reading, if you are thinking of adopting a dog, think again, and think once more. Research the breed, and consider your budget. Dogs are not cheap. Literally thousands can be spent at the vet. They may get diseases or illnesses that require medicine. Make sure you have realistic budget for a dog. Know how to take care of it. Make sure if you do adopt, you spay or neuter your dog (or cat).

Thousands upon thousands of animals are put to sleep each year because the parent dogs were not spayed or neutered. There are clinics that will do this at a lesser charge. Make sure you have the space for the type of dog you are adopting. Make sure the dog fits your personality. If you are not energetic, do not get a golden retriever! If you do not like small dogs, don't get a Chihuahua.

The Internet is full of websites containing all the information you need to know about each breed, including their expected size, temperament, energy level, life expectancy, etc. Bookstores have shelves upon shelves of educational material as well. Do the research. You (and your dog) will be happy you did.

Appendix B

Buddy's Favorite Treats:

Michael and I just thought we'd share some of Buddy's favorite treats. If you have a dog, try these out at snack time in lieu of regular dog biscuits (or if you are looking for a really good bribe for your dog). Just make sure to check with your veterinarian before giving your dog any new or different food or snacks.

1. Carrots- Usually given in place of a regular dog biscuit. A little bit healthier of a snack—but do not tell Buddy that!

2. Peanut Butter on Crackers- Take any type of cracker and smear a little peanut butter on it. Do not put too much as it gets difficult for the dog to swallow it—even though it could be amusing to watch! This is typically given to Buddy when we are too lazy to take him for a walk, in hopes that he will forgive us and forget all about it.

3. Cheese- He likes any type, alone or on a cracker. Usually given after Buddy behaves for a while, such as when he has been quiet for more than ten minutes at a time.

4. Tuna- All-time favorite. If Buddy is ever hiding somewhere in the house, all we need to do is open a new can of tuna. He'll be by our side within seconds. We give this to him straight from the can. No mayo needed! (We just remove it from the can first so he does not cut his tongue on it.)

5. Bananas- This is actually Brandi's favorite treat. While Buddy and Toffee never turn down a banana, Brandi will intimidate us with her intense staring until we give her some.

6. Plain White Rice- Though plain and bland, this is still one of Buddy's favorites. This also serves as a helpful digestive aid when his tummy is not feeling too well.

Enjoy!

ALSO WRITTEN BY ELIZABETH PARKER:
Unwanted Dreams

What if the life you were living was not the one you were meant to live?

One man. One moment in time. One horrific night. That was all it took.

Alexandra had married the man of her dreams and they had their whole life ahead of them. They had a wonderful marriage, a beautiful house and essentially they could not be happier. Things were falling into place as intended, until one beautiful evening turned devastatingly tragic.

The catastrophic events that transpired ensured that none of their lives would ever be the same. Faced with an impossible moral decision, Alex had to make a choice that would come back to haunt her in years to come, once again forcing her to tempt the hands of fate.

How does a random murder shatter the many lives of those within the killer's path? How do you pick up the pieces of your life when unforeseen circumstances alter your future forever?

Unwanted Dreams provides just the right amount of twists and turns, leaving the reader in suspense, pondering the following question: How strong is the bond that exists between families and how far would you be willing to go to save your own?

*A portion of the proceeds from the sale of this book will be donated to a dog rescue organization.

PHOBIA

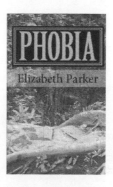

Growing up with phobias that have terrified him his entire life, Matt Brewer had finally made the decision to go to counseling, seeking help once and for all.

He entrusted his emotions in the hands of strangers and depended on them to help conquer his fear. What he did not count on was having his fears become a distinct reality, leaving him fighting for his life and the lives of those around him, including his girlfriend whom he intended to marry.

Tortured and bound, he comes face to face with evil with no one to hear his screams. Time is of the essence and it's a literal race against the clock in order to make it out alive.

*A portion of the proceeds from the sale of this book will be donated to a dog rescue organization.

Final Journey
Buddys' Book

After the publication of "Finally Home," Buddy was diagnosed with terminal cancer. Once the unthinkable happened and Buddy's precious life was cut short, his family was left heartbroken and devastated.

At the same time, in another state, poor economic conditions forced another family to give up their golden retriever.

As fate would have it, his name...was Buddy.

While they were mourning the loss of their beloved dog, another dog was mourning the loss of his treasured family.

Brought together by misfortune, they entered each other's lives to help put back together the pieces of their broken hearts.

This story is for both Buddys, producing the subtitle "Buddys' Book."

A portion of the proceeds from the sale of this book will be donated to an animal rescue organization.

Evil's Door

Childhood rumors are often prevalent in a family-oriented community. Some boast that they have seen a UFO flying overhead while others claim to have witnessed a ghost soaring through the trees. Some stories are so believable that they trickle down from sibling to sibling, friend to friend; creating a neighborhood buzz that lingers for years.

Ryan Sheffield's neighborhood was no different. Though no one would admit it, adults and children alike were freaked out by the eccentric woman who lived in the ghastly corner house, but aside from that, his world as he knew it was an ordinary one.

Bizarre situations did not surface until Ryan began working at his very first job. To his peers and superiors, it was just a traditional office. To Ryan, it was much more than that after a series of inexplicable occurrences haunted his every conscious moment.

Through a bit of intense research, he uncovered the building's gruesome history and was led down its horrifying path. He opened the door to a hell he did not want to live in and tried his best to avoid the evil that surrounded him. The truth revealed itself to him in more ways than one; a truth he was better off not knowing and one that could essentially end his life.

12106396R00105

Made in the USA
Lexington, KY
23 November 2011